Blue-Collar Leadership®:
Leading from the Front Lines

Mack Story

DEDICATION

To those who make it happen on the front lines everyday.

You matter!

And, I believe in you.

CONTENTS

ACKNOWLEDGMENTS

I would like to thank the many blue-collar leaders on the front lines that have impacted my life in ways they will never know.

Two of the greatest lessons I learned from front line leaders:

1) Give credit to others when things go right.
2) Take responsibility when things go wrong.

Many of the best people I have ever met were wearing safety glasses, ear plugs, a pair of well-worn, dirty, greasy, steel-toed boots, and a smile. I'm glad to have met you all. You're an amazing group of hard-working, dedicated people that matter. You deserve to work with a great leader. It's my hope that you become one.

Each of you have played a small part in shaping my thinking and therefore my life. I will be forever grateful. Thank you!

1

I'M ONE OF YOU

WHO WE ARE MATTERS

"A few start at the top, but most of us start at the bottom."
~ Mack Story

Merriam-Webster's simple definition of blue-collar: requiring physical work; relating to or having jobs that require physical work.

I'm proud of the many years I spent on the front lines as part of the blue-collar workforce in various manufacturing plants. Those years, and the many outstanding people I worked alongside, shaped me and prepared me to be uniquely positioned to help you today. For that, I'm forever grateful. But, I'll never be satisfied.

If you'll learn and apply what I'll be sharing with you on these pages, you won't have to settle any longer. Like me, you should always be grateful but never be satisfied. You can become a lot more. It's a choice I hope you will make.

You have unlimited potential within you and can move far beyond your current circumstances. I want to help you increase your influence. When you increase your influence, you'll have more options no matter where you work or what work you do.

Those on the front lines have been overlooked for far too long. I've written this book for you. If you invest your time in reading it completely, *you will benefit tremendously.*

When you decide to accept responsibility for your future,
you will be able to define your future.

My intent is to motivate and inspire you to climb to the next level and beyond. I want to help you go faster and farther by sharing what I didn't begin to learn until nearly 20 years after my first day on the front lines. I wish someone had given me this very book in 1988. Things would have been better for me. And, they would have been better much sooner.

I hope as you make your way through this book you begin to see things, including yourself, in a much different way. I hope you feel encouraged, empowered, and engaged to make a bigger difference in your own life and those around you. I believe you can do things you've never even imagined doing.

I want to take you back to my days on the front lines for a moment. I'm sure you will be able to relate in some way. You may not work in the manufacturing plants like I did. But, if you're a blue-collar worker, I know you work hard and long, no matter what type of work you may be doing: electrical, plumbing, construction, farming, mining, manufacturing, oil & gas industry, carpentry, service work, welding, assembly, etc.

There are many of us. We are everywhere.

The blue-collar workforce built this country;
they can and must help save this country.

I worked long, hard hours, in hot, cold, dirty, and sometimes, unsafe environments while being bossed by others who thought they were far above me because they had a position of authority and power or simply because they had a college degree. Most often, I only respected the position and not the person. They had to earn my respect.

They didn't listen to me. They didn't have to. They didn't want to. However, if I wanted to continue to get paid I had to do what they said, when they said it, and how they said it.

I didn't realize I had a choice. But, I did. You do too. This entire book is going to help you realize you have a lot of choices and a lot of untapped potential.

I'll never forget my first day on the front lines in 1988 at the age of 18.

It was the first time I had been in a manufacturing plant of any kind in my life. I was quickly taken from the front office and handed off to someone in front of a very large, loud, and oily machine, a machine like nothing I had ever seen before. I had been in the plant for about 10 minutes at that time.

It was official. I was a blue-collar factory worker. I would stand in front of many machines for many years in many different plants before that would change.

I was shown how to load the machine, start the machine, unload the machine, inspect the parts, and repeat. Then, I was on my own. I was at work doing exactly what I was told to do.

When I got home from work, all of my clothes, even my underwear, were soaked with oil. It was that way for the next two weeks until someone finally told me I could purchase a plastic apron in one of the break rooms, for less than a dollar, that would help keep me dry.

This is how my blue-collar career started.

For the next 10 years on the second and third shifts, I often worked seven days a week, 10 to 16 hours a day for months at a time to make ends meet. When overtime was available, I was always quick to volunteer. I didn't want to. I needed to.

I was greedy because I needed to be greedy. Life was tough. I could never get ahead regardless of how many hours or days a week I worked. I'm sure not much has changed today for many who are still making it happen day in and day out on the front lines of the blue-collar workforce.

There wasn't much respect for us then, and there's not much respect for many on the front lines today. I know the potential that lies within you. It was also within me, but I didn't know it. I want to help you realize it sooner rather than later.

Everything changed for me in 1995 because one person believed in me and shared that belief with me.

It will be my privilege if I can be that person for you today.

I want you to know: I respect you.

I want you to know: Who you are matters.

I want you to know: I believe in you.

2

I BELIEVE IN YOU

MOTIVATION COMES FROM THE OUTSIDE, BUT INSPIRATION COMES FROM THE INSIDE

"The dictionary defines belief as trust, faith, and confidence. However, that definition is selfish and requires judgment. I think we need to change the way we believe in people. We need to redefine the way we believe in people. We should redefine belief as encouragement, empowerment, and engagement. This definition is selfless and doesn't require judgment." ~ Joshua Encarnacion

You may be wondering, *"How can Mack believe in me? He doesn't even know me."* Well, my intent on these pages is to express my belief in you in the way Joshua defined belief in the quote above, as selfless and without judgment. I like to refer to this type of belief as *"unconditional"* belief which is similar to unconditional love.

When we believe in someone or love someone unconditionally, it simply means we believe in them or love them because they are people, not because they behave or act in a certain way. *I do believe you can make your life better.* Believing in someone unconditionally is a choice. It's a choice that builds trust and strengthens relationships.

Since I don't know you, I can't trust you, have faith in you, or have confidence in you based on what I know about you. That would be based on conditions or *"conditional"* belief. However, I can easily have unconditional belief in you. But, when we work with others and depend on others to get the job done, it's too easy to become selfish, judgmental, and base our belief in them on specific *conditions* being met first.

I want to share a real example from my life where a stranger *unconditionally* believed in me. It not only changed my direction, but it also changed my life. I share this story in more detail in my first book, *Defining Influence: Increasing Your Influence Increases Your Options*.

It was 1995. I was 25 years old. It was around 2am. I was wearing old, dirty jeans, an old t-shirt, greasy steel-toed boots, safety glasses, earplugs, and an old, dirty blue jean apron hung around my neck. As usual, I was at work in the middle of the night when most people were home sleeping soundly with their families.

I operated a large drill press and a CNC lathe machining holes in steel parts. It was a dirty, boring job, but it paid the bills. I was in the middle of what would become a three month streak of working 12 plus hours a day for seven days a week without a day off. Long hours and weekend work were a normal part of my life on the front lines.

On that particular night, there was a corporate industrial engineer from our headquarters observing me. He was there to do a time observation study. I was surprised because he could have done what he had to do on the day shift.

He informed me the Plant Manager (PM) had asked him to work with me because I consistently recorded high production. As I worked, the engineer observed me. After we got to know each other a little, he told me the PM believed I had the potential to be more than *"just a machine operator"* if I would apply myself and get some additional education.

The stranger had no idea I barely graduated high school.

Throughout the night, he expressed his belief in me and continued to do his best to get me to see my potential. He had no idea. I wasn't interested in going to college. Not me!

I didn't plan to ever go. I knew who I was and what I wanted. I didn't need anyone, especially a stranger, telling me what I needed to do to advance in the company. What did he know about me? He knew I had potential. He knew it. I didn't.

I had never seen him before and never saw him again. He has no idea how his words impacted me. He inspired me to become intentional about changing my life.

I thought it was just another night in the grind on the front lines. But, something happened. I started thinking differently. He had planted a seed of *possibility* inside of me. I hope I can plant that seed in you.

I began to ask myself many questions: What if I went to college? What would change? Should I do it? Could I do it? How could I do it? When could I do it? Then, I did it.

I took action and enrolled in the local community college the very next semester. I decided to officially rescript my life simply because a stranger had unconditionally believed in me.

"We already live with many scripts that have been handed to us, the process of writing our own script is actually more a process of 'rescripting,' ... As we recognize the ineffective scripts within us, we can proactively begin to rescript ourselves." ~ Stephen R. Covey

I started college, as a single parent, while working long hours and weekends to make ends meet. I didn't enjoy high school, so volunteering for more schooling was a big sacrifice.

It took me nearly five years to get my first two year degree, but I did it. I was paying the price to change my circumstances. *I did have potential.* I did not have to keep doing the same thing for my entire career. When I began to change my thoughts, my life began to change. I was slowly moving away from being a reactive, negative person and was becoming a more proactive, responsible person.

If you want things to change, you must change the way you think. And no, you don't have to go to college to live better.

"The reason so many people never get anywhere in life is because when opportunity knocks, they are out in the backyard looking for four-leaf clovers." ~ Walter P. Chrysler

3

YOU'RE IN THE PERFECT PLACE

YOU'RE EXACTLY WHERE YOU'RE SUPPOSED TO BE BUT NOT WHERE YOU HAVE TO BE

"An educated person is not the one with the most knowledge, an educated person is the one who is willing to reflect, evaluate, and modify his most cherished beliefs when a new idea comes along." ~ Christian Simpson

There's a story about a tourist who paused for a rest in a small town in the mountains. He went over to an old man sitting on a bench in front of the only store in town and inquired, *"Friend, can you tell me something this town is noted for?"*

"Well," replied the old man, *"I don't rightly know except it's the starting point to the world. You can start here and go anywhere you want."*

The same is true for you and me. No matter where we are, we can start and go anywhere we want. Will it always be easy? No. Will it always be possible? Absolutely, *if* we're willing to pay the price.

Obviously, very few people start at the top. But, we don't all have that in common with those lucky few. However, what we do have in common is this: If we want to move forward from wherever we are, we all must start.

"Most people fail in the getting started."
~ Maureen Falcone

I agree, some do *"fail in the getting started,"* but I think the bigger issue is *failing to keep going* once you have started.

If you're on the front lines like I was when the engineer believed in me and inspired me to get started *again*, that's where you start if you want to get to the next level and beyond. You're in the exact place you need to be. You're at the starting line. Getting to the starting line in life is easy. All you must do is step up. Then, you must choose to run.

> *It's much easier to go from failure to success
> than it is to go from excuses to success.*

This book is going to help you think in a way that will allow you to get started or, if you're already started, keep going. It will also accelerate your thinking.

You had to get started at some point to be where you are. It didn't just happen. You didn't end up there by accident. Like it or not, you ended up there by choice.

If you want to move up in the company or move forward with your life in general but feel stuck wherever you are, I've got good news. You haven't run out of choices. You're simply not making the *right* choices.

Why? I have no idea. Only *you* can answer that question.

When you think of why you're stuck, don't make excuses. Excuses are like exits when you're traveling along the highway to success. Excuses don't take you where you want to go, they take you someplace you don't want to go.

> *An excuse is simply a choice
> not to do what you know you should do.*

I want to give you something to think about whether you're stuck or not. If you're not stuck, use it to help someone that is.

Most of the time people quit growing and going when the *price* gets too high. Many people are not willing to part ways with the toxic people in their lives or sacrifice their time and/or their money to continue moving forward to the next level. Growth usually requires a lot more *time* than money, so *not having the money is just another excuse.* And most often, it's not even about our time. *It's about our choices.*

Before you get too deep into this book, I want to help point out a few key choices I hope you will make as you're reading and thinking your way through it.

I encourage you to look at this book as a *tool*, not a book. A tool you can you use immediately to identify areas in your life you may need to change. A tool you can use in the future when reflecting on changes you have already made or changes you weren't ready to make initially but will be ready to make eventually.

Whatever you do, **DO NOT GIVE IT AWAY!** I made that mistake when I first started reading leadership books. I didn't realize the value of keeping them and revisiting them, especially my highlighted key points. Today, no one gets any of the hundreds of leadership books I've read. I may give away new ones, but not the ones I've read and marked up.

You should personalize this copy by marking it up in a meaningful way, underline key points, fold the pages when something on a page really has something meaningful you want to revisit and reflect on. And most importantly, write down some of your own thoughts about what you are reading and what you may need to do differently.

Once you've finished it, if you know someone else will benefit from reading it, and you believe in them, show them by buying them a copy as a gift, but don't give them your copy. Sure, they could read it and give it back. But, to get the most out of it, they will need to personalize their copy, make it their own just like you, and be able to reflect on it later.

Have you ever wondered why people don't do the things that seem to be common sense? Things like we've just covered like *get started* or *keep going*. It seems like common sense to me.

"If we refuse to become a leader because we don't believe we can get to the top, we are limiting ourselves from reaching our potential; and we are limiting the impact we can have on others." ~ Ria Story

4

COMMON SENSE IS NEVER ENOUGH

COMMON SENSE MEANS WE UNDERSTAND WHAT SHOULD BE DONE, BUT ACTUALLY DOING IT OFTEN REQUIRES UNCOMMON SENSE

"We only truly know something—that is, have personal knowledge of it—when we can apply it to get results."
~ Polanyi

As you continue reading, I'm sure you will often find yourself thinking, *"This is all just common sense."* It is commonly *understood*. However, when it comes to human behavior, what's commonly understood, often referred to as common sense, is most often not commonly practiced. If it was, there would be no market for leadership and people development, and everyone would be amazingly happy and tremendously successful.

But, leadership is a *HUGE* industry! Many people are unhappy at work and at home while struggling to make ends meet. Nearly all of them know something they should *stop doing* to improve their lives and know something they should *start doing* to improve their lives. But, they don't do it! Why?

Common sense alone will not lead you to success. It will help, but it's not enough. Knowing and doing are two very different things that will lead you to very different results. Knowing how to lose weight doesn't mean someone who wants to lose weight will lose weight. We all know how to lose weight. We watch our calories in (what we eat) and exercise (calories out).

It's common sense. Everyone knows that!

To know something and not do it is not truly knowing it.
To understand something and not apply it is
not truly understanding it.

Everyone seems to know common sense is not common practice. However, most people don't seem to know why.

Knowing why common sense is not common practice requires an intellectual level of understanding far beyond common sense. In other words, you need to be an above average thinker.

When I speak on the subject of common sense in my leadership development seminars, everyone in the room always realizes the leadership principles I speak about are common sense. They also know they are not commonly practiced by most people.

Why isn't common sense always common practice?

I've come to understand the problem is found in the definition of common sense which leads to our expectations sometimes not being met. When someone says something is common sense, they mean it is commonly understood.

What most people are missing is this: There's a huge difference between *understanding what should be done* and *doing what is understood.* And, it often takes more smarts to do something than it does to understand something.

Doing what is commonly understood
often requires uncommon sense.

Here's a simple example to prove my point:

It's common sense to understand you should invest your time and money into your own personal growth and development if you want to become more effective and successful at work which will also improve your life when you're at home. Do you agree? If you want to be better, you need to get better. Common sense right? Of course, it is.

But, are you doing it frequently and regularly? You're doing it now as you read this book. Is this your first personal development (leadership) book or one of hundreds? Do you think the person reading a leadership book for the first time is getting the same results as someone that has read hundreds of leadership books? It's *highly* unlikely.

Leadership is influence. The more influence you have the more options you will have at work and at home. Who will get the promotion, the person with the most influence or someone else? Who will have a more enjoyable day at work or at home, a person with more influence or less?

"The top 5 percent of achievers invest an average of $3,000 per year on personal growth while the other 95% average only $7 per year." ~ Les Brown

If we invest in ourselves and become intentional about moving ourselves forward, we *will* move forward. Our personal and professional lives *will* get better. Most people will instantly agree. But, most people don't do it. Most people won't do it.

Instead, most people will choose to waste more money on a weekend hanging out having a good time than they will invest in their own personal growth and development in a whole year.

Why is this the case? Because common sense means we understand what we should do. However, doing it requires *uncommon sense.* I'm sure by now you get the point. After all, it's common sense.

I added this chapter because I want to be sure you realize up front **it will take much more than common sense to apply what you will learn in this book.** You must develop and use uncommon sense to get the results you deserve and are capable of achieving. Don't just zip through the pages. What I share is easy to understand, but it's not so easy to apply. Think deeply about what you're learning and the impact applying it will have on your life.

You *can* apply it. But, *will* you apply it? I hope you do!

"The critical skill of this century is not what you hold in your head, but your ability to tap into and access what other people know. The best leaders and the fastest learners know how to harness collective intelligence." ~ Liz Wiseman

5

THERE IS AN "I" IN TEAM

EVERY TEAM IS MADE OF "I"NDIVIDUALS

"I'm just a plowhand from Arkansas, but I have learned how to hold a team together – how to lift some men up, how to calm others down, until finally they've got one heartbeat together as a team. There's always just three things I say: 'If anything goes bad, I did it. If anything goes semi-good, then we did it. If anything goes real good, they did it.' That's all it takes to get people to win." ~ Paul "Bear" Bryant

Paul *"Bear"* Bryant was one of the greatest college football coaches to ever lead a team of young men down the field. He was also a *"plowhand"* from Arkansas. A blue-collar worker. The blue-collar world has produced some of the greatest leaders of all time, so you should be proud and hold your head high. *Without them, the world as we know it would not exist.*

There's nothing holding you back but you. As my blue-collar friend, Donovan Weldon, stated so well, *"The only person between you and success is you. MOVE! The only person between you and failure is you. STAND FIRM!"* Those are strong words of wisdom. Donovan started on the bottom just like you and me. But today, he's the CEO of Donovan Industrial Service in Orange, TX near Beaumont.

Donovan's success didn't happen by accident. He made it happen. You can make things happen too! He's a blue-collar leader that believes in and develops his team on a regular basis. I know because my wife, Ria, and I had the privilege of being brought in to speak to his team about leadership in 2014. They are making it happen on purpose for a purpose!

It's time for you to stop playing small and start playing tall.

A college degree is not required for you to play at a higher level. Not having one is simply an excuse some people use to continue playing small. If you want a college degree, use what you will learn on these pages to find a way to get one. If you don't want a college degree, use what you learn on these pages to make it happen without one.

You are the key to your success. You must believe in yourself. You must grow and develop yourself, which is what you're doing as you read this book. Do not stop growing! And when the time is right, you must bet on yourself.

Understanding your role as a team member is another must. Those on the front lines often underestimate themselves because they can't see the big picture. They can't see the value they have to offer. Far too often, their boss isn't a high impact leader and needs a lot of growth and development too. Bosses are often given the title without any formal development.

When I write about the front lines on these pages, I'm not only talking about the people in entry level positions. They are obviously on the front lines, but they also have leaders that are on the front lines with them and various team members supporting them too. They can all learn from these pages.

This book was written specifically for anyone at any level that visits, interacts with, or works on the front lines.

The principles I share with you must be applied if you want to make a high impact and be recognized for leading from the front lines. Regardless of your position, the more you apply these principles, the more options you will have, and the more positions you will be offered as you climb even higher.

Teams are made up of "I"ndividuals, so there are many I's on every team, regardless of how many times you hear, *"There is no 'I' in TEAM."* As a matter of fact, *you are one of them.* Every person on a team is an "I" and has the potential to lead (influence) the team, positively or negatively.

"Leadership is influence. Nothing more. Nothing less."
~ John C. Maxwell

You must understand there are many official and unofficial teams in the organization where you work. They are very dynamic and constantly changing.

When most of us think of which team we are on, we immediately think of our peers, the ones on the same crew, in the same department, or working on the same job. This is our core team, but it only represents the smallest team we're on. We also support other teams too, as others support our team.

When we choose to contribute beyond our immediate team, we are choosing to be part of a bigger team. Often, this only requires a choice to do so. Your choice to get involved in other areas sends a clear message to the high impact leaders.

When you play tall, you choose to contribute because you know it will increase your influence and your impact on the front lines. If you want to play tall, you should want to be noticed, to be selected, to volunteer, to share information, to accept more responsibility, and ultimately, to make a contribution at a higher level.

As a direct result of your choice to step up, your influence increases. You're demonstrating you can lead from the front lines and will be seen and respected by all high impact leaders as a high impact leader. Your actions will not go unnoticed.

When you play small, you choose not to contribute because you don't want to do more. If your goal is to coast until pay day, it won't be a secret you can keep. When you make every effort not to be noticed, not to be selected, not to volunteer, not to share information, not to accept responsibility, and ultimately to not contribute, *you will absolutely be noticed.*

As a direct result of your choice not to step up, your influence decreases. Your influence on the front lines and with your leaders will be diminished. You are more likely to become reactive and frustrated blaming others for what you have chosen. Blaming others will further reduce your influence.

You first make your choices, then your choices make you.

"The most valuable player is the one that makes the most players valuable." ~ Peyton Manning

6

BE BETTER TOMORROW

WHEN YOU BECOME MORE VALUABLE, YOU WILL BECOME MORE SUCCESSFUL

"If you have too little confidence, you will think you can't learn. If you have too much, you will think you don't have to learn." ~ Eric Hoffer

I'm writing this book to help those who want to develop positive influence with their team and their leaders because they aren't content continuing to do the same things the same way for the rest of their career.

I assume if you're still reading you want to be more, do more, earn more, and have more.

If this is the case, your goal shouldn't be to simply go to work and do your very best to play it safe. Your goal should be to go to work and make the biggest, most positive impact with and for your team. Not some days, everyday.

Think about it. If you were the coach, which player would be more valuable? The one who performs well by themselves? Or, the one who performs well and helps others perform well?

Remember when you were a kid playing some type of team sport with friends, and it was time to pick teams? Who got to pick? The two kids with the most influence. Who did they pick first? The kids they believed could and would help the team win.

Life is no different. The best team players, in the eyes of those doing the picking, get picked first. There's nothing more important to your future than doing something every day to be better tomorrow than you are today.

This simple principle is why I started reading about process improvement (Lean Manufacturing) in 2005. Then, I began reading leadership books daily in 2008 and plan never to stop. It's the one thing I know I can do today to be sure I'm better tomorrow. Although I'm no longer on the front lines, this principle still applies. As a result, I'm now doing things I could never have imagined when I was on the front lines.

Focus on becoming more valuable, not more successful.

The only person you need to be better than tomorrow is the one you are today. It's that simple.

Your family and your company need you to play at the next level and beyond. Before you can do that effectively, you must master the level you're at now. Too many people want to be somewhere else which is great, but they haven't demonstrated and shown mastery at their current level yet. Their focus is on going fast, so they go slow. You need to go slow, to go fast.

"Take the time it takes, so it takes less time." ~ Pat Parelli

There's a question you need to start asking yourself today. It's a question I will be asking myself regularly for the rest of my life. It's about beginning with the end in mind.

Since I first heard the question, I have never stopped asking it, answering it, acting on it, or sharing it with others. It's the guiding force behind my personal growth. This question has allowed me to move from wondering and wishing, to being and doing. It has shaped, and continues to shape, my life.

Every one of us is someplace. However, most of us want to be in a different place. Most of us are uncertain about what to do to move from where we are to where we want to be.

The question I'm going to share assumes you know where you're going. If you don't know, you need to nail down the answers to the following two sets of questions first.

This first set of questions will establish your starting point: Who am I? And, where am I?

The second set of questions will establish your destination:

Who do I want to become? And, where do I want to be?

They also reveal a gap. I call this the *"Success Gap."* The gap between where you are and where you want to be.

Here's the question you need to learn to ask yourself:

Will what I'm about to do move me in the right direction?

This question is packed full of potential just like me and you!

The question is important.

The answer is more important.

But, your actions are most important.

It's a simple concept actually. If the answer is yes, you do it. If the answer is no, you don't do it. It says easy, but it does hard.

When you ask the question, the answer is yes, and you follow through, you close the gap. When the answer is no, but you do it anyway, you widen the gap.

Will what I'm about to do move me in the right direction?

I use this question for big, life changing events and small, everyday decisions. I used this question when I decided to write this book. Ria and I actually discussed the answer together. There were many things I could have done, but what was most important relative to moving me in the right direction? At that moment, it was writing this book.

As you grow and change, your values are also defined and refined. As a result, what would have been a *"yes"* in the past may become a *"no"* in the future. Or, what was a solid *"no"* in the past may become a burning *"yes"* in the future. Things you once valued may simply fall away without much sacrifice as you make more focused decisions and reap the rewards of doing the right things at the right time for the right reasons.

The most important person you will ever talk to is *yourself.* So, be careful what you say. Likewise, always be intentional about what you ask yourself because you'll be the one responsible for answering the question.

"It is the capacity to develop and improve themselves that distinguishes leaders from followers." ~ Bennis and Nanus

7

THE SECRET TO YOUR SUCCESS

YOU GET PAID BY OTHERS,
BUT YOU WORK FOR YOURSELF

*"When you take charge of your life, there is no longer a need
to ask permission of other people or society at large.
When you ask permission, you give someone veto
power over your life." ~ Albert F. Geoffrey*

I'm about to share the *inside scoop* with you: the secret to success. As you read this chapter, keep the chapter on common sense in mind. Actually, you need to keep that chapter in mind throughout this book, but especially here because *uncommon sense* is needed to get the full *value* out of what I'll be sharing.

Who do you work for? Think about it. Understanding your answer matters, and it matters a lot.

When I'm speaking to groups on leadership, one of the questions I often ask them is, *"Who do you work for?"* Immediately, people begin to shout the name of the company where they work. Some with great pride and others simply because they think that's what I want to hear.

It's always instantly clear to me they haven't thought much about the answer to the question or the impact the answer has on their choices day in and day out while they're at work.

I believe this will most likely be an eye-opening and key chapter for you as you begin to *see* things differently.

Once the shouting dies down, I follow up saying, *"I didn't ask, who is paying you to work? I asked, who are you working for?"*

Someone else is always paying you to work, but you are always working for yourself. This is true whether you own your own company or whether you work at someone else's company. If you weren't working for yourself, you wouldn't expect to be paid.

For some reason, it's easy for others to see that people who own their own business are working for themselves, but so is everyone else when you really think about it. And, you *really* need to think about it.

When people understand they are working for themselves, they have a different mindset. They see themselves as the business owner and everyone else as customers, potential customers, and/or as potential advertisers telling others about their business through *word of mouth* referrals. Everyone agrees *word of mouth* is the *best* type of advertisement.

They expect to serve the customers who are paying them to work, not be served by them. They care what customers think about doing business with them. They *intentionally* do a better job because they know it matters. They care how they make their customers feel because their customers will determine how well their business does in the future. Will it grow or will it slow? They want more business and as much positive *word of mouth* advertising as possible. Who wouldn't?

You most likely work at a company owned by someone else. However, if you accept a payment for the service/labor you provide, you are definitely working for yourself. Let that sink in for a minute.

You *are* in business for yourself because *you are working for yourself.* Your product is physical labor mixed with shared ideas.

For many, this is an odd way to look at yourself and your job. No matter how odd it may seem, if you apply uncommon sense, it is crystal clear. As a result of this new discovery, your view on everything about your job and those you work with should be reconsidered. What needs to change?

The lessons in this book will now be even more important. That's a small example of how being aligned with the proper reality can change your thoughts. When your thoughts are aligned with reality, you are much better positioned to build stronger relationships and achieve amazing success.

If the light bulb hasn't gone off yet, let me help you. What this means is **everyone you interact with at work is either a customer, potential customer, and/or a potential advertiser** spreading either positive or negative *word of mouth* advertisement about your business: YOU.

"To generate good profit, it's critical not only to understand but to anticipate what customers value, their expectations, measures, incentives, needs, alternatives, and decision-making processes." ~ Charles G. Koch

This also means your boss is your #1 customer. He or she can help you or hurt you the most.

Do you treat them as your #1 customer? If you do, things are probably pretty good for you. If you don't, anyone with common sense will know things may not be so good.

What type of *word of mouth* advertising is being spread about your business (YOU) throughout the organization by your boss and all of the other people you work and interact with?

All of those people will talk to others about you and how you serve them as *customers*, just as you do to others. When they are interacting with you for any reason, they are your customer. Just like when a business owner provides complimentary service and hopes the non-paying customer will, at a minimum, give positive *word of mouth* advertisement, this is what happens every day on the front lines. People talk about other people.

How you serve your paying and non-paying customers has a major impact on your promotions, your raises, your influence, your options, your growth in the company or your termination from the company, and ultimately, your future working in other departments or even other companies.

How you operate, *your* business, matters. And, *it matters a lot!*

"The key to moving beyond average is doing what exceptional people do, not wanting what they have."
~ Mack Story

8

SOMEONE IS ALWAYS WATCHING

YOU ARE ALWAYS TEACHING WHAT YOU'RE MODELING, REGARDLESS OF WHAT YOU ARE TEACHING

"Nothing is more confusing than people who give good advice, but set a bad example." ~ Norman Vincent Peale

"Nothing is more convincing than people who give good advice and set a good example." ~ John C. Maxwell

Modeling is not a word I remember ever hearing during my many years on the front lines. I think the concept of modeling should have been taught to us on the front lines which is why you find yourself reading about it today. You are a *role model* whether you want to be one or not because someone is always watching.

Think for a moment about the front lines. Which type of role model will have more options, more opportunities to advance and grow, more influence among the leaders? A positive role model or a negative role model? One embracing change or one resisting change? One offering new ideas and suggestions for improvement or one that isn't? Or, one that's just there to get paid or one that's there to make a difference? *Who you are matters.*

It's common sense, but as you now know it's not common practice. There's often a lot of resistance to everything new and different by some on the front lines. Those resisting change usually don't have very much influence with the high impact leaders, only with others who believe what they believe.

However, there are a few that embrace change and new

things. They have a lot of influence with the high impact leaders who are responsible for moving the organization forward. Which team would you want to be on? A team moaning and groaning with little or no influence? Or, a team with leaders that want your help, have a lot of influence, and can help shape your future? Again, common sense right?

You would think these front line team members that step up are admired and respected by all of their peers. However, they are often ridiculed by some for *"brown-nosing"* or *"sucking up"* because they are making the others look bad.

Do not let average people keep you from becoming exceptional. Some will try very hard to hold you back. Don't let it happen. Keep intentionally moving forward.

You're not really making them look bad. They're making you look good by not stepping up themselves. If they look bad, it's their fault, not your fault.

It happened to me from day one and continued until I left the front lines because I made things happen, and I helped the leaders make things happen. I didn't simply want to be on their team. I wanted to be the MVP! I was on a mission to grow my business: ME.

The result: I was promoted 14 times in 20 years while working on or supporting the front lines. I want to help you get the same or even better results by giving you a head start.

Remember, you're working for yourself. So, be sure to represent yourself well to your #1 customer: the boss.

Apply what's on these pages, and you'll be amazed at the future you will create. A future you can't begin to imagine now. There are opportunities in your company right now that you and others can't see. I'm asking you to prepare for those opportunities without knowing what they are.

If you want to see ahead in the dark, you must first turn on the light. Then, if you want to see even farther ahead, you must start moving slowly in the direction you think you want to go. As you move, you will begin to see the previously unseen.

Your growth is exactly the same. You're holding in your hand a way forward, if you'll turn the light on and start moving in a new direction.

Here's a story I couldn't have imagined when I was on the front lines loading and unloading machines trying to make ends meet.

In 2013, Ria and I had the privilege to join John C. Maxwell in Guatemala City, Guatemala for the *"Transformation Begins with Me!"* cultural transformation initiative.

We helped John and 150 others train more than 20,000 Guatemalan leaders in just under three days. We also attended a special event with the President of Guatemala at the Presidential Palace. Without applying the principles in this book, we would have never been there. As I've said, they can change your life in ways you can't understand at this moment.

On the first day of training, Bertha (my 20 year old interpreter) and I were assigned to train approximately 50 high level business leaders. While in the taxi on our way there, I was sharing leadership principles with her. I wanted her to know I saw her as much more than *"just an interpreter."*

I wanted her to know I saw her as a young leader on the front lines with a big role to play in the transformation of Guatemala.

As we walked into the room to get set up, Bertha looked at me and said, *"I don't know if I want to be a role model Mack."* I tilted my head a little and looked at her sincerely and replied, *"Bertha you already are because someone is always watching you. The real question is not, 'Do you want to be a role model?' but rather, 'What kind of role model will you be?'"*

I could tell she was in deep thought for several minutes after my comments. I knew she was considering the principle behind modeling. We talked more about this later when we had a chance. I wanted to be sure she understood we influence other people through our actions whether we intend to or not.

You may never know how or when your actions have influenced others or if your influence was positive or negative.

"Example isn't another way to teach,
it's the only way to teach." ~ Albert Einstein

9

YOUR POTENTIAL IS UNLIMITED

YOU SHOULD ALWAYS BE GRATEFUL, BUT NEVER SATISFIED

"When we fully develop our potential, we create superior value for others – and that in turn helps give meaning to our lives...Life is pretty empty without passion for what we are doing. What a tragedy to reach the end of your life and only be able to say, 'I got by without having to do too much.'" ~ *Charles G. Koch*

The way you see the world has a lot to do with how the world sees you.

I've seen far too many front line workers come to work unsatisfied, irritated, and negative. And sadly, they often leave the same way. I worked alongside many of them for years. We did the same job. I loved mine. They seemed to hate theirs.

They simply didn't like coming to work, being at work, or working for that matter. They were last to get going at the start of the shift and first to get finished at the end of the shift. They were also first to leave for break and last to return from break. What they were modeling didn't go unnoticed.

They were not on a mission heading somewhere. They were on a job headed nowhere.

I know there are still many just like them today. There's an old saying that goes like this, *"If Bob has a problem everywhere Bob goes, then Bob is the problem."*

"There are no problems we cannot solve together, and very few that we can solve by ourselves." ~ *Lyndon Johnson*

Too many people can't see they are the problem. In one company where I supported those on the front lines for several years with Lean Process Improvement and Leadership Development, I remember a person who was not happy about her job.

We were in the middle of a one week Lean Leadership Certification class where I taught many of the principles I'm sharing here and many that I'm not. There are far too many to put in a small book like this or any single book for that matter.

She came up at one of the breaks as many of those in my classes often do. She wanted to tell me something she had been thinking about after hearing some of the leadership lessons. She had been reflecting on who she was and where she was. I'm sure she had already heard me talk about Bob and Bob's problem, which was Bob.

She proceeded to tell me how she had worked there at the company for many years, but she was unhappy before and left for another job. When she got her new job in a new company, she was happy at first, but she said she quickly became unhappy again, so she asked to return to her old job.

They rehired her and a few years later, she was standing with me in the leadership class, unhappy again.

She went on to tell me before coming to my class she was actually once again searching for a new job at a new company. But that morning, she had opened her eyes and realized she was the problem because everywhere she went she had a problem.

As a result, she was now perfectly positioned to deal with the problem that was causing her all of these problems. She proceeded to tell me she had decided to stay because she now knew she would also be unhappy at her next stop no matter where it may have been.

She decided at that moment to be grateful, but not satisfied. She decided to change what needed to be changed: herself.

"The secret of change is to focus all of your energy, not on fighting the old, but on building the new." ~ Socrates

26

A year later, we talked again. She said things were a lot better. She was glad she stayed because she felt better too. She also expressed appreciation the company had invested in her by having me there to teach her about leadership.

They invested in her. She responded and chose to demonstrate her appreciation by investing in the development of herself. Life was better for her, her teammates, and her leaders. Because they were better, the company was better.

"Business should not be about elites serving other elites; it should be about giving all of our people ways to develop and express their unique gifts. Every person has such gifts; great leaders know how to uncover them." ~ Bob Chapman

If your company provided you with this book, it's because they care about you. They are *investing* in you. But, they can't make your life better, only you can do that.

Being always grateful means you choose to appreciate everything about your life and your job. You must choose to be grateful for the job, for the boss (your #1 customer), for the team, for the pay, for the benefits, for the things having the job allow you to do and have, and most importantly, for the opportunities to grow yourself while working in someone else's company. That's a privilege.

I've always seen every job as you should, a place to learn, grow, and make a difference. I've always thought to myself, I can't believe these people are paying me to train myself for my next job, to make a bigger difference.

Remember, always be grateful, but never be satisfied.

I've never been satisfied and never will be. But, I've also been grateful and always will be. It's all about being positive about where you are and where you're going. It's a choice.

"The purpose of life is not to be happy. It is to be useful, to be honorable, to be compassionate, to have it make some difference that you have lived and lived well."
~ Ralph Waldo Emerson

10

FOCUS ON THE MIRROR

THE FACE YOU SEE LEAST IS YOUR OWN

*"A man's environment is a merciless mirror
of him as a human being." ~ Earl Nightingale*

This was one of my weakest areas in my early years on the front lines. I don't mean a little weak. I mean extremely weak.

I should have been fired many times, but I wasn't. They probably kept me on the team because I was one of the most productive team members in the entire plant. I loved making process improvements and keeping the machines running. But, I'm not happy to tell you I had too much pride and ego in my twenties and thought I was better than everyone else.

I complained all the time about those who weren't *"pulling their weight."* I should have been helping them instead of blaming them. But, I needed help myself. It took me two or three years on the front end to figure this one out.

I don't get a do over. I wish I did. But, I hope I can help others struggling to realize they have blind spots too.

We all have blind spots. And believe it or not, the biggest blind spot we all have can be found in the same place. Where is it? It's always between us and the mirror. The face we see least is *truly* our own.

We don't know about ourselves what we need to know about ourselves. Think about that for a moment and consider the impact it has on your life and your results. Think about the story I shared in the last chapter about the unhappy woman. She had a blind spot, and it was making her miserable. For many years, she was the problem and didn't even know it. We all have the same problem: ourselves. I am my problem. YOU are your problem.

She tried changing the easy thing, her place of employment. But, she was still miserable. So, what did she do? The same exact thing. She changed her place of employment again. She was doing what we all tend to do, changing what was easy to change. Although I'm sure if you could ask her, she would say it didn't seem too easy at the time. However, things didn't change for the better until she changed herself.

> *You must change what needs to be changed,*
> *not what is easy to change.*

I'm also sure if you could ask her today she would say changing herself was, and continues to be, much harder than changing her work address.

Unfortunately, we don't see ourselves as others see us. We don't see ourselves as we are. If we did, most of us would immediately start making changes to address those things on the inside that are holding us back on the outside.

What people see you do, along with what they feel because of what you've done or are doing, ultimately determines the level of influence you have with them. When it comes to work, your influence determines what type of work you do, who you work with, where you work, when you work, and how much you get paid to work. *Who you are matters.*

Your level of influence with others will determine who you attract (personally and professionally), what they trust you to do with them or for them, when and if they want to associate with you for mutual benefit, and most importantly when and if they want to help you. *Who you are matters.*

Let's say, I'm a material handler in a manufacturing operation. I'm driving the forklift bringing and taking away materials to your work area. I have a boss (my #1 customer), and you have a boss (your #1 customer). Your #1 customer is also my customer, my #1 customer is also your customer. We are also each other's customer. And when we do business together, those watching are potential customers and definitely *word of mouth* advertisers. They will either say positive or negative things about us based on what they see and feel as we interact with each other.

Here's the scenario: I've just pulled into your work area to take away something I think is ready to go. When I arrive, I see you're not ready for me just yet and could use some assistance. Do I get off my forklift and help you because I understand you're my customer and everyone is watching? Or, do I think to myself, *"It's not my job."*

One choice will build trust with my customers. One choice will create distrust with my customers. More trust equals more influence. Less trust equals less influence.

In this scenario, the material handler choosing to get off the forklift to assist the customer will be praised and talked about positively. The material handler choosing to sit impatiently on the forklift and wait for their customer to complete the tasks alone will not be praised and will receive negative *word of mouth* advertisement from those watching.

Do you think these choices will impact production, morale, relationships, people's opinions of you, etc.? Do you think one choice is more likely to lead to promotions, recognition, and appreciation? Do you think one choice is more likely to lead to ridicule, blaming, and finger pointing?

I could write thousands of examples for anyone in any industry. You are not exempt. Every day, you are either getting it right or getting it wrong. You are either building trust or creating distrust with each of your *customers*. You are either moving forward or backward as a result. In either case, it's not their fault. It's your fault. *We can choose our actions but not the consequences that come from our actions. All of our choices matter.*

If you're not advancing as quickly as you think you should be, what are you not doing that you should be doing?

Our problem is not out the window (others). It's in the mirror (self), we just have trouble seeing it.

"The moment you take responsibility for everything in your life is the moment you can change anything in your life."
~ Hal Elrod

11

THE POWER OF THE PAUSE BUTTON

WHAT HAPPENS TO YOU IS IMPORTANT, BUT YOUR RESPONSE TO WHAT HAPPENS TO YOU IS MOST IMPORTANT

"Self-mastery is the hardest job you will ever tackle. If you do not conquer self, you will be conquered by self. You may see at the same time both your best friend and your worst enemy, by simply stepping in front of the mirror."
~ Napoleon Hill

From the hundreds of books I've read and thousands of hours of audio I've listened to, all related to leadership and personal growth and development, the principle behind the pause button is the single most important principle I have ever learned. This one principle alone changed my life.

If I had known about it in 1988, my climb up the ladder from the front lines would have started much sooner and been much quicker. It took me years to even get one foot on the ladder, much less start climbing it. I had A LOT to learn.

Between stimulus and response, there is a space. And in that space, humans have the ability to pause and choose their response. I learned this from my first leadership book, *The 7 Habits of Highly Effective People* by Stephen R. Covey. Those words changed me instantly.

The fact I could choose my response to any stimulus had never crossed my mind. I was a very reactive, fly off the handle type of person. I used to say having a short temper runs in the family. What I discovered that day was irresponsibility runs in my family and a lot of other families too.

When I teach about stimulus and response, I refer to the

pause button we all have. What I mean is this, we each have the ability to pause and choose our response when something happens. We cannot always control what happens to us, but we can always control our response to what happens to us.

We all respond to stimulus. Proactive people respond based on values in alignment with natural laws and principles. But, reactive people (short tempered like I *used* to be) respond based on feelings. Often, they don't pause at all. They just react instantly to the feelings inside them like I did in the past.

Let's look at an example from my days on the front lines.

It never failed, when I had planned something for the weekend, which was anytime I wouldn't be able to volunteer to work the weekend, there would be times when I would be told at the last minute I needed to work. Like many others on the front lines with me at the time, I would get angry.

I was told to work overtime (stimulus) which I needed, and I still instantly got angry (response). In those days, I didn't know I had a pause button. I had never even considered my values much less made a conscious decision to pause, consider them, and respond based on them. It happens instantly today.

But back then, things were different. My response was instant and based purely on my feelings. The feeling I didn't want to work since I had plans not to work. The feeling this happened all the time. The feeling if they knew what they were doing we wouldn't have to work, or at least they could have given me some notice. The feeling they could care less about me or my plans. And on, and on….

My results were also much different back then. Because of my constant personal growth and development, today I can earn more in a few hours speaking on leadership than I used to earn in an entire year on the front lines. I don't say that to impress you. I have no need to impress you. I say it to motivate and inspire you to consider making some changes.

I always tell people, if you want dramatically different results, you must do things dramatically different. For many that read this book, applying the principles I'm teaching will be dramatically different.

If what I'm teaching you seems totally different than how you normally operate, I'm here to tell you *big things* are waiting for you *if* you're willing to make some *big changes*. I know because I have transformed my life with these simple to understand but hard to apply principles. You and your family are worth the effort. Make it happen!

As I improve the man in the mirror, my results improve. Common sense right? But, doing it requires uncommon sense.

Many people are so reactive they won't even consider nothing makes them mad other than themselves. If they can choose to be mad, they can also choose not to be mad. We've all told the lie, *"So and so makes me so mad."* That's nothing but a lie. Many believe it to be truth. But, there are some people out there that know better. Being mad is a choice.

Back to the overtime issue. What would I do differently now?

First of all, I would understand I choose to walk through the door every day knowing how the company operates. Nobody makes me come to work. I would own that choice and all that comes with making it. I would always be positive.

I would consider the impact my behavior has on my #1 customer (the boss) and the impact he/she has on my future here and maybe even someplace else. I would know even if I don't get along with my boss (I'd be working on that too, maybe it's because I always complain about everything), it's bigger than the relationship with the boss because other people are watching. Maybe, other bosses I would rather work with are watching or listening? But, because of the behavior they see and the *word of mouth* advertisement they hear from my boss in their closed door meetings, the other bosses have zero interest in working with me. I'm not even on their radar screen.

What would I do? I would rearrange my schedule without a complaint. The more we complain the less we obtain.

"If you do what is easy, your life will be hard. But if you do what is hard, your life will be easy." ~ Les Brown

12

THE FUTURE IS IN YOU NOW

IF YOU DON'T CHOOSE YOUR FUTURE, SOMEONE ELSE WILL

"There's nothing you have to do. We all have the power to make a decision that will direct us to a new destination. Each of us can make a choice that will change our life."
~ John G. Miller

Your future really is in you now. That's not just a play on words. It's the truth. Your future is defined and refined by the choices you make every day.

You can't predict your future, but *you can create your future.* This is powerful and profound if you have never taken the time to slow down and truly think it out. This may be hard to grasp, so let's apply it to the last example about the last minute request by the boss (#1 customer) to work overtime.

Let's consider some options to see how I could create a different future purely based on my choices.

If I don't use my pause button and simply choose to get angry because I'm being told one more time I must cancel my plans and work overtime, I would create a future of frustration, bad working relationships, and become a bad role model for those around me. I may not get the next promotion or the next raise and may eventually lose my job because of my lack of cooperation and my negative influence on the team.

Something else would also happen. Those agreeing with me would support and encourage me. They would be angry too. We would stand around and talk about the boss, the company and how much we hate being yanked around. Then, we would do it again for the next two days while we were working the

34

overtime. We may rebel and keep our productivity low over the entire weekend, and if we're really upset, the next week too.

As a result, I strengthen my relationship with those like me while damaging my relationship with my boss (#1 customer) and any other high impact leaders that are watching. I also fire up everyone else around me at break and lunch causing an overall production loss which may actually lead to me and my followers having to work the next weekend too. If so, I wouldn't accept responsibility. I would simply choose to repeat the cycle of blame. That would be the future I created.

However, if I used my pause button and responded based on values, I wouldn't get angry because I chose to work there knowing this happens regularly. I would also know I valued not working weekends. As a result, I would want to be a positive influence and help the boss keep everyone motivated and inspired to stay productive in an effort to do all we could do to help catch up, so we wouldn't have to work next weekend too. Instead of blaming, I would be helping.

As a result, I would strengthen my relationship with my boss and increase my influence with all the high impact leaders that had expected the worst from all of us but didn't get it from me. I would hear all of the rumblings and try to help everyone see how our behavior can make it better or worse. Some would start to talk bad about me because I wasn't angry and upset. I would be okay with that too because I would understand I'm working for myself, and my actions impact me and my family the most.

If I truly didn't like it and didn't want to work the weekend, I could quit because I would also know I have that choice too. I can do whatever I want, however I want, but I also know I must live with the consequences.

If I wasn't prepared to quit and was simply angry, things could get worse for me and my family in an instant, especially if I didn't give a notice. That could impact my ability to get the next job.

If I was prepared to quit, I could move on without any worries. But, I would stay positive, work the weekend, and work out a two week notice because I know how I leave one job can greatly impact my ability to get the next job.

That was a lot of ifs, but they could all be real choices along with many others I didn't mention. The point was to help paint you a picture of how what we choose to do creates our future. The thousands of choices we make every day of our life, not only shape our life, but create our future.

With only a few exceptions, you're exactly where you're supposed to be based on all of the choices you have made leading up to this moment. If you were supposed to be someplace else, you would already be there. You must own the results your choices have produced.

Until you own that you're responsible, you're being irresponsible. That's the reason those blaming others for their circumstances can't improve their circumstances.

How ridiculous is that thought process? It's my fault, but I'm going to say it's your fault. And then, when you don't fix something that only I can fix, I'm going to blame you for that too while thinking all of this will somehow improve my circumstances. That thought process has a zero chance of making anything in your life better. Many people wake up and live out this model from start to finish every day.

Working on the front lines is tough at times. I seldom had the privilege of working a normal five days a week, 8 hours a day job. What I didn't understand was how my choices literally made things better or worse for me. I was simply reacting based on my feelings.

Think about your job and the day to day choices you make. What impact are they having on your future? Where are you heading? What choices (good or bad) did you make in the past that have led you to where you are today? If you want tomorrow to be better, make better choices today. The hardest person you will ever lead is reading this book right now.

"We are anxious to improve our circumstances
but unwilling to improve ourselves.
We therefore remain bound." ~ James Allen

13

COURAGE IS CONTAGIOUS

COURAGE ALLOWS AVERAGE PEOPLE TO ACHIEVE EXCEPTIONAL RESULTS

"Life shrinks or expands in proportion to one's courage."
~ Anais Nin

For many, the missing piece of the puzzle is courage. Courage to do the right things at the right time for the right reasons while those around you are constantly trying to get you to do the wrong things for the wrong reasons.

Even in my early years on the front lines, I didn't like to see others being treated unfairly. As an infantry Marine, I had plenty of courage to stand up for anyone I thought was being treated unfairly or to anyone else I thought was wrong or doing something wrong.

However, I didn't seem to have the courage to stand alone when I should have. I would always stand up for what others convinced me was right. I hadn't yet learned to think for myself. I hadn't read a book like this or heard anyone in my life talk about the principles I'm sharing with you on these pages.

Eventually, my choices almost cost me my job.

I would regularly let my fellow front line team members talk me into doing things I shouldn't have been doing. They knew I had a short temper at the time and would use it against me. Our boss would do or say something, the next thing I knew I was fuming because of what the others were saying, not because of what he said. Today that makes no sense to me at all. But, I also know it's still happening on the front lines daily.

I was allowing them to influence me. Next thing I knew, they had talked me into confronting the boss on behalf of the team. I actually kind of enjoyed it. I shouldn't have, but I did. At the time, I didn't know any better.

Usually, I would end up paying the price in frustration and lost influence while the others stood in the shadows without any skin in the game. I wasn't too bright in those days. I was like a puppet on a string. My teammates played me like a violin because I let them. They looked like angels, and I looked like the devil. Some probably thought I was.

I was always very productive and got along with people for the most part as long as they left me alone. I was young and ignorant. I let people of all ages in all positions push my buttons. When they did, everyone saw the worst of my short temper. It was ugly, and I'm not proud of it. I didn't know what I didn't know. I had a lot to learn and a lot to unlearn.

I assume my consistently high productivity was the only reason they kept me. Either way, if they had fired me, I would have deserved it without question. Fortunately, they never did. They gave me chance after chance along the way. For that, I am grateful.

Even way back then, I was also never satisfied. I wanted to learn new jobs, accept more responsibility, and prove I could outperform anyone on any machine, with quantity and quality. I was on a mission. I wanted to climb the ladder.

Of course, I was going about it all wrong, but I didn't know that. I was about to find out though. I didn't realize who I was mattered more than what I knew.

Not too long ago, I visited with the man who was my Plant Manager at the time to give him a copy of my first book, *Defining Influence*. I knew he would be proud to know I was doing something positive with my life.

I got to know him during my 14 year career in his plant. The times I've been describing were my first year or two there. Working nights, I didn't get to know him personally.

He is now long retired, a little over 80 years old, full of energy, and doing great. During my visit, he was anxious to share a story about a meeting he had with me while I was still struggling with self-control in those early years. At first, I didn't remember the meeting at all. Unfortunately, it started to come back to me as he started sharing the details.

I had been involved in several issues as a front line employee early in my career under his leadership. At that point, it was time for him to take action. It was time for me to shape up or ship out. He stayed late, asked the HR Manager to stay late, and called me and my supervisor into a meeting.

He said he intended to be, and was, very hard on me in the meeting in an effort to help me grow or go. He said he was very surprised and impressed by how polite I was during the meeting considering all he had heard about me and my short temper. Finally, he gave me a choice: resign or straighten up immediately. I got it right. I told him I would straighten up. He said, *"Well, get out there and get to work."*

I did and instantly started to be a better employee. My integrity has always mattered. When I say I will do something, I do it. He cared for me then and cares for me now. I could feel it that day, and I could still feel it during our recent meeting. He's a great person and made a big impact in my life.

One interesting thing he mentioned to me during my visit was I had called him one year after this incident. He said no one had made a call to him during his entire career like the one I made. I called him back exactly one year later on the anniversary of the meeting to thank him for giving me one last chance and believing in me when I didn't believe in myself. I had called to confirm with him I had made the changes he requested and intended to continue to improve. He agreed I had and was impressed with my call and my turnaround. He still is to this day.

He had the courage to do the right thing. Often, courage is contagious. I think I caught a little of it while I was in his office. As a result, I had the courage to create a better future.

"While one person hesitates because he feels inferior,
another person is making mistakes,
and becoming superior." ~ Henry C. Link

14

YOU ATTRACT WHO YOU ARE

THOSE WHO LIKE YOU THE MOST
ARE THE MOST LIKE YOU

"The people with whom you habitually associate are called your 'reference group,' and these people determine as much as 95% of your success or failure in life."
~ Harvard Social Psychologist, David McClelland

Your friends in your personal life reveal a tremendous amount about who you are at the core. Likewise, those you associate with most at work also reveal a lot about what kind of team player you are and where you're headed or not headed.

Do you hang around the trouble makers, the coasters, or the game changers? It's a secret you can't keep. Everyone knows. They will always know. Every player knows which team the other players are on.

Who you are is who you attract. It's a law of influence. You can't fake who you are for very long. The game changers don't want to hang around the trouble makers, and the trouble makers don't want to hang around the game changers. It'll never happen because they don't have the same values.

If you want to change teams, you must change what you truly value. Even then, it will take time because you must prove yourself to those in the new group who will be measuring you based on your actions, not your words.

I've heard it said in many different leadership training seminars that we become the average of the five people we voluntarily hang around the most. I absolutely agree. That's why I don't hang around with anyone voluntarily that isn't on fire, meaning they are focused on intentional growth and personal development.

When I first heard we become the average of the five people we hang around the most, it caught me off guard a bit. I had never really thought about it.

But, it's true. We start talking like they talk, acting like they act, dressing like they dress, eating what they eat, drinking what they drink, doing what they do, and most importantly, we begin to think like they think and believe what they believe. They don't determine us because we will always have the freedom to choose our response to any stimulus.

However, they can absolutely influence the choices we make if we choose to be around them.

"One of the most expensive things you could ever do is pay attention to the wrong people." ~ Henry Cloud

Before the Plant Manager nearly fired me, I was hanging around the instigators and the trouble makers. You can easily guess my behavior. I was one of the worst. After my decision to get onboard, I chose to stop hanging around those people.

For some time, I didn't hang around anyone at all. It's often lonely for a while when you transition to a group with higher level character. You must completely leave those with less character behind in order to build trust with those that have developed more character. They may let you interact, but they want to see a proven track record of real change before you're really on their team. Therefore, you must travel alone for a while.

This is the hardest part for most people. They don't want to travel forward alone. As a result, sometimes they go back to where they come from. When they do, nothing changes.

I ate my lunch at my machine and worked through my breaks for many months after nearly being fired. It was a wakeup call for me. I was only 21 or 22 at the time.

I was on a mission, and I wanted everyone to know I was moving in a direction of my own choosing. I kept to myself as I began searching for myself and trying to figure things out.

As you know, the front lines in the blue-collar world can be pretty rough, especially on the youngsters. I had a young son and wife at home. I didn't need to lose my job. I needed to get a raise and eventually a promotion. I had something to prove to myself and to the leaders (the decision makers). So, I wanted my transformation to be drastic. It was. Everyone noticed.

I discovered I didn't really know who I was without the influence of the instigators and troublemakers. In my Marine Reserve Infantry Unit, I was among elite game changers from all walks of life, blue-collar and white-collar. Actually, we all had green collars. They lifted me up and made me better. They were completely different than the instigators and trouble makers which brought me down and made me worse at work.

In the Marines, I received two meritorious promotions during the same time I was nearly being fired from my civilian job on the front lines. Good or bad, influence can be powerful.

It's obvious looking back, I had a different group of five at each job. This really validates this principle. I was the same person but was being influenced in different ways at each location. Therefore, I got very different results at each job.

If you truly want raises and promotions, take a look around at those closest to you at home and at work. Wait until you finish this book because you will be looking through a different set of glasses. You will have a new insight on what you need to change in yourself and in your life.

Unfortunately, those closest to us are often holding us back. I'm sure you've had to leave some people behind to be where you are today. As we grow, develop, and move upward, we must be willing to leave those that don't want to grow with us behind. It doesn't mean we're better than them, or we don't like them. It simply means we're going in a different direction. If you and I are heading in two different directions, we can't ride together.

"In the end, you may not be able to change the people around you, but you can change the people you choose to be around." ~ John C. Maxwell

15

CHARACTER COUNTS

WHO YOU ARE ON THE INSIDE IS
WHAT OTHERS SEE ON THE OUTSIDE

"Character is like a tree and reputation like a shadow. The shadow is what we think of it; the tree is the real thing."
~ Abraham Lincoln

Merriam-Webster's definition of character:
• the way someone thinks, feels, and behaves: someone's personality
• one of the attributes or features that make up and distinguish an individual
• the complex of mental and ethical traits marking and often individualizing a person, group, or nation
• main or essential nature especially as strongly marked and serving to distinguish
• moral excellence and firmness

When it comes to character, remember this. If you fake it, you won't make it. This applies on the front lines and in your personal life. Your character will determine which groups you're attracted to and which groups are attracted to you.

You may have noticed nearly all new team members start out strong. Then, something happens, and many seem to go downhill. This is because as time passes their character comes to the surface which allows them to connect with and associate with the others like them. Next, that group's influence magnifies the best or the worst in them.

You may have seen people who get hired for what they know, but later, they get fired for who they are. Nothing will hold you in place or move you backward more than your own character. Nothing will propel you forward and upward faster than your own character. *Who you are matters.*

Poor character was my problem during those early years on the front lines. My climb upward started out slow. Actually, I wasn't climbing at all. I was stuck, simply wandering around the base of the mountain blaming everyone else because I wasn't climbing the mountain. I didn't *fully* understand what I'm sharing with you now until nearly 20 years later.

You're getting a tremendous head start on me and many others who haven't read this book regardless of their position. Use it to move far beyond average. You will learn character is what separates the exceptional from the average.

You can see right through someone faking it when it comes to caring for you whether it's an upper level manager, a boss, or a co-worker. When it comes to your character, it's not about what you know. It's about who you are.

Others can also tell if you're faking it or if you're truly sincere. Your level of influence with them depends on what they feel from you. Do they truly feel you value and support them? Do they feel they can trust you? Do they feel you care?

Character is the key. When it comes to building strong, effective, long-lasting relationships, no one really cares how much you know until they know how much you care.

Who you are on the inside is what people experience and feel on the outside.

I define high impact character as: thinking, feeling, and acting in a congruent way while making excellent moral and ethical choices based on self-evident natural laws and principles.

Mahadev Desai, Mahatma Gandhi's secretary, when asked how Gandhi could speak for hours, without notes, while mesmerizing his audiences said, *"What Gandhi thinks, what he feels, what he says, and what he does are all the same. He does not need notes. You and I, we think one thing, feel another, say a third, and do a fourth, so we need notes and files to keep track."*

Desai was describing what it means to be congruent. Gandhi walked his talk. His actions matched his words in everything he did. He was real. He was a whole person.

It's all about modeling. You must work constantly to align your words, actions, and beliefs with natural laws and principles. Your ability to live in harmony with these natural laws and principles, which are shared throughout this book, determines the level of trust you are able to build with others along your growth and development journey.

When you do what you say you will do or live how you say you will live, do you build trust or create distrust? Will you develop more or less influence if you walk the talk (congruency)? If you don't walk the talk?

What you think you will do is important. What you say you will do is more important. But, what you actually do is most important.

Once you go public with your thoughts, you have made a commitment or promise to be or do something. Now, you either demonstrate congruency, or you don't. Will you walk the talk? *Will you build trust or create distrust?*

Do you keep commitments? Do you care who you are? Do you care what you say? What impact are you having on your ability to influence others? What talk do you walk?

People with the *exact* same skill sets and abilities will achieve a wide range of results. Some will be poor. Some will be rich. Some will have no options. Some will have many options. Some will be promoted. Some will be demoted.

What's the difference if the skill sets and abilities are the same? The *difference* is the individual's *character.*

Character is personal, but it's not private. Everyone who knows you has an opinion about the kind of person you are.

> *"Our reputations do not come from how we talk about ourselves. Our reputations come from how others talk about us." ~ Simon Sinek*

16

CHARACTER TRUMPS COMPETENCY

WHO YOU ARE MATTERS
MORE THAN WHAT YOU KNOW

"You can't climb to the top of the mountain with base camp character." ~ Mack Story

Character counts because it serves as a *multiplier* of your competency.

You have far more than you need to succeed on the outside because it's provided for you. The question is do you have what you need to succeed on the inside? In this area, you are fully and completely responsible.

In my more than 20 year career, I've never been fired. I probably should have been early in my career when I was reactive, but my high productivity, second chances, and my ability to change on the inside saved me.

I can't imagine being hired, then later, being fired. But, it happens. I've witnessed it countless times. I've even had to hire people I later had to fire.

To understand why most people get fired, consider why most people get hired.

Typically, people are hired for what they know (competency). They get hired to do a job. This is where the problems often start. There's much more to being a great team member than being able to do the job.

Why are they hired? They have a great looking resume. They have great answers to all the questions. Their skill set matches the job requirements. They may have even gotten verifiable results in the past. They meet the educational requirements. They have solid referrals. So, they're hired.

Then, day after day, week after week, month after month, what they know is confirmed. However, something even more important is also revealed through their choices, their actions, and their reactions. As time passes, everyone begins to learn who they are (character). Who they are matters.

Assume what they know (competency) meets or exceeds expectations. That's usually true. However, if they don't know what they need to know, most often, they can usually learn what they don't know in a timely manner and continue to be employed. Or, their leaders may find a better fit for them. Competency is seldom an ongoing issue. I can't recall anyone I know being fired due to their competency.

If competency isn't the problem, what is?

Who we are, *our character*, is the source of most of our problems. It's why most people are fired. When it comes down to it, who you are matters much more than what you know.

- How do you deal with things that don't go your way?
- Are you reactive or proactive when it comes to change?
- Are you part of the problem or part of the solution?
- How do you treat others? How do you make them feel?
- Do you talk behind their backs?
- Do you give others credit? Do you take the credit?
- Do you want to serve or be served?
- Do you show up at work on time? Or, are you late?
- Are you on time for meetings? Or, are you late?
- Do you do what you say you will do?
- Do you do it when you said you would do it?

Remember, what's *common sense* isn't always common practice. It often takes *uncommon sense* to get it right.

"We hear of businesses succeeding or failing, but it is not the business ... it is the people who succeed or fail."
~ Truett Cathy

What's the solution? How do you move forward instead of backward? You must learn and apply the principles in this book and many other leadership books.

When you get it right, you move forward. When you get it wrong, you move backward. The key is knowing every choice you make will either move you forward or backward. When it comes to your character, there is no such thing as standing still.

Many companies invest most, if not all, of their time and dollars developing the competency of those on the front lines which means there are little or no resources invested in the area of character development (leadership training).

This doesn't mean the leaders are bad people.

Sometimes really good people, just like the rest of us, simply don't know what they don't know. You may not have ever known or thought deeply about what you're now learning. That doesn't mean you were a bad person before. It just means you didn't know what you didn't know. This happens to me every time I read a book. It never ends. You were a great person before you read this book. But, you'll be better after.

If your company provided this book to you, that's a big deal. They care about your character development. You can increase your influence by personally thanking the leader.

If your company didn't give you this book, don't blame them. Help them.

You now have a chance to be recognized as a high impact front line leader by sharing it with a boss/manager/leader already modeling much of what you're learning on these pages. They will listen. They will also be impressed you have read this book! Use your influence to get the company to provide copies to all of those on the front lines. Here's your chance to make an impact at the next level.

Those organizations investing their time and dollars in character-based people development attract the best (character) and the brightest (competency). Not sometime, all the time.

"A sign of wisdom and maturity is when you come to terms with the realization that your decisions cause your rewards and consequences. You are responsible for your life, and your ultimate success depends on the choices you make."
~ Denis Waitley

17

LEADERS HAVE FOLLOWERS

THE DIFFERENCE BETWEEN A LEADER AND A BOSS IS WHAT THEY VALUE

"A leader is someone who has followers. If there are no followers, there is no leader. A person may have subordinates, workers, admirers, associates, co-workers, friends, and people who report to him or her, a person may have authority over other people, a person may hold an elective office, and a person may influence a large number of people, but that does not make that person a leader if there are no followers." ~ Jimmy Collins

If you're like most people on the front lines, when you read this chapter, you're going to naturally start looking out the window at your boss or manager. It's just what we do. Don't do it, unless you can do it without blaming them.

"Many people suffer poor health not because of what they eat but from what is eating them. If you are harboring any ill will or resentment or grudges, cast them out. Get rid of them without delay. They do not hurt anybody else. They do no harm to the person against whom you hold these feelings, but every day and every night of your life they are eating at you." ~ Norman Vincent Peale

If you're looking out the window to find someone to help, by all means possible, find some people to help regardless of whether or not they have a position of authority. But, this chapter is not about the people out the window.

It's about looking in the mirror. It's about you. What you're learning isn't only about work. It's also about knowing whether you're a boss or a leader at home.

It's about helping you learn the difference between a boss and a leader, so you can make the choices that will allow you to *"create the future"* you desire. Do you want to be a boss or a leader? Bosses value position and power over others (formal authority). Leaders value positive influence with others (moral authority).

You, *and your children or spouse if you have either,* can actually feel the difference between a boss and a leader. You don't have to be a leadership expert to be able to determine if a person is a boss or a leader. You just have to spend some time with them. The difference is how they make you feel.

A boss makes you feel used. A leader makes you feel valued.

A boss makes you feel bad. A leader makes you feel good.

A boss makes you feel dumb. A leader makes you feel smart.

A boss makes you feel like it's their idea. A leader makes you feel like it's your idea.

A boss makes you feel powerless. A leader makes you feel powerful.

A boss makes you feel guilty. A leader makes you feel responsible.

A boss makes you feel small. A leader makes you feel tall.

A boss makes you feel afraid. A leader makes you feel brave.

A boss makes you feel alone. A leader makes you feel supported.

A boss makes you feel weak. A leader makes you feel strong.

A boss makes you feel defeated. A leader makes you feel invincible.

A boss makes you feel tired. A leader makes you feel inspired.

A boss makes you feel like an object. A leader makes you feel like a person.

Now, let's look out the window on purpose for a minute.

As a child, were your parents bosses or leaders? Maybe one was a boss and one was a leader? Or, were they both bosses or both leaders? Remember, leading yourself well isn't just about what happens at work. It's also about what happens at home.

If you're a parent, now look in the mirror. What do your children see when they look at you? Look at the list again. How do you make them feel? *Do you care how you make them feel?*

Others always know when you truly believe in them. Not because of what you say but because of how you make them feel. Every day on the front lines you are also bossing or leading. Bossing is about telling. Leading is about selling.

People feel a certain way every time they interact with you. When they feel good, your influence increases. When they feel bad your influence decreases. Consider the impact on your *word of mouth* advertisement and the future you're trying to create.

If you are a formal front line leader with others reporting directly to you, what do they see when they look up at you? How do you make them feel? *Do you care how you make them feel?* I *know* it matters how you feel when you look up at your leader. I *hope* it matters how you feel when you're looking down at work and at home (if you have children) too.

You may not be able to change the leader you report to, but you can always change the leader your team (or children) reports to. Be the leader you want to see others be.

Leading others is about the choices you make. It's not about a title or position you are given.

Now for the most important question: Regardless of whether or not you have a position of authority, when you are working with others, do you fit the profile of a boss or a leader? If you are not sure, refer to the boss/leader list again.

"A true leader has the confidence to stand alone, the courage to make tough decisions, and the compassion to listen to the needs of others. He does not set out to be a leader, but becomes one by the equality of his actions and the integrity of his intent." ~ Douglas MacArthur

18

POSITIONS ARE OVERRATED

IF YOU CAN'T LEAD WITHOUT A POSITION, YOU WON'T LEAD WITH A POSITION

"The cost of leadership is self-interest."
~ USMC Lt. General George Flynn

I've added these few chapters on leaders, position, and followers because if you learn to lead without a position, it will only be a matter of time before you are recognized for your influence and offered a formal leadership position.

Then, it will be your choice to accept or deny that position based on the future you're attempting to create. *Will the position move you in the right direction?* Sometimes, yes. Sometimes, no.

You will always have more options when you can lead (influence) people without a position. Why? Because your influence is real. It's authentic. People actually *want* to follow you. They don't *have* to follow you. It's not tied to or related to a position of formal authority. It's based on *who* you are, not *what* you are. That's *moral authority*.

Think with me for a moment.

If you were the big boss, and you were going to promote one of two supervisors to a higher level leadership position and everything else was equal, would you be more likely to promote the supervisor people follow only because they have to? Or, the supervisor people follow because they truly want to? Which supervisor has more influence? It's a no brainer, right? *Moral authority is very powerful.*

I've spent my entire career leading with moral authority. I've only had three people report to me directly in my entire career which spans nearly 30 years. However, I get paid to speak, train, coach, and write about leadership. Why? It's because I don't need a position to make things happen. All I need is a team! You have a team too. Are you ready to lead?

Your value is multiplied when you can lead without a position. Trust me. I know. I've transformed entire organizations without a position and been paid very well to do it. I have experienced amazing results with amazing front line people during my entire career. Even when I was just like you on the front lines, I was leading and making things happen without a position. I didn't need one and really didn't want one. *Positions are overrated.*

Don't focus on becoming more successful. Focus on becoming more valuable. Don't focus on getting a position. That's playing small. Focus on growing and developing your influence (leadership). That's playing tall.

"In periods where there is no leadership, society stands still. Progress occurs when courageous, skillful leaders seize the opportunity to change things for the better."
~ Harry Truman

This entire book is about helping you grow and develop your moral authority by helping you learn to lead from the front lines. You can do it. I know because I did it for years and loved it. And, I did it without a book like this to help me. I had to learn it the hard way, by trial and error with very few high impact leaders to model for me what you've been learning.

Today, I have logged over 11,000 hours leading cross-functional, front line, blue-collar teams through various types of organizational change. Most often, the team members hardly knew each other or me. I didn't have any formal authority over any of them. I was an outside consultant usually only working with each team for one week.

They could make me or break me. They didn't have to do anything I said. If I couldn't quickly build trust and gain influence, we simply wouldn't complete the project. As a result, I wouldn't have been asked to come back.

That never happened. We always achieved amazing results

together. I developed moral authority with them quickly. I learned from them, and they learned from me. I was often able to influence them to do things their boss or other leaders, with a position, couldn't get them to do. You can always make things happen when you have moral authority.

Leadership is influence. Nothing more. Nothing less. The person with the most influence at any given time for any given reason is the leader of the pack. Not sometime, all the time.

When someone is given a position of authority over others, they are really being given *"artificial"* influence. Artificial influence will make a *boss* with a position think they are a *leader* because they confuse respect for their position with respect for them as a person. Moral authority turns a boss into a leader.

Artificial influence creates the illusion that you actually have real influence. However, if you choose to influence people using only artificial influence, you are not leading. You are simply bossing. Sure you can accomplish a lot bossing others, but what are you leaving on the table? What could a leader do?

Bosses make things happen with people who *have* to help them. Leaders make things happen with people who *want* to help them.

A boss thriving on artificial influence (position) isn't interested in developing himself or the other bosses on their team. That's what leaders do, not what bosses do. If you want to lead from the front lines and beyond, continue to do what you're doing right now. Don't stop growing and developing yourself. You are worth it. It will be easy to separate yourself from the crowd if you begin *applying and teaching* what you're learning. *Applying it and teaching it will make you a leader.*

"The only influence that truly has any meaningful value is based on moral authority, not formal authority. Position or title isn't important or required. Fear and intimidation doesn't exist. Others choose to follow you because of who you are and how you make them feel." ~ Mack Story

19

FOLLOWERS CHOOSE LEADERS

ALL GREAT LEADERS WERE
FIRST GREAT FOLLOWERS

"To excel in leadership, you must first master followership."
~ Truett Cathy

As one of my mentors, John Maxwell says, *"Leadership is influence. Nothing more. Nothing less."* I realize I have written this many times, and you will see it again because I want it to stick. *You have influence. Therefore, you are a leader.* In case you missed it, leadership is influence.

Considering this definition, we are all leaders. But there are different levels of leaders, different styles of leaders, and different designations for different types of leaders. One of the many designations of a leader is *follower.* Confusing right?

How can that be? Well, it gets complicated, but here's a simple illustration. No matter who you are or what position of authority you do or do not hold, if I choose to follow you, I am a follower. At the same time, regardless of whether or not I have a formal position of authority, if someone chooses to follow me, I am a leader. *People can be following and leading at the same time.* However, there are different levels of followers and leaders on two different scales: positive and negative.

I also share a little more about followers in my book, *10 Values of High Impact Leaders.*

The best leaders know when it's best to lead and when it's best to follow. They know and understand leadership is very dynamic. They know following allows others to lead.

There is nothing wrong with being a follower. If you are a follower, then be the best follower you can be. *We must be great followers before we can choose to become great leaders.* If you're content with following, meaning you don't want followers, you should spend a little time reflecting and asking yourself, *"What am I leaving on the table?"* More importantly, *"Why am I choosing not to increase my influence with and through others?"*

You are fully capable of climbing the leadership ladder and increasing your influence which will increase your options. If you aren't working to increase your influence, why aren't you?

> *Influence is the only thing that will move you forward.*
> *Everything rises and falls on influence.*

By definition, a follower is also a leader because they also influence others. However, the term follower represents a lower level leader on the leadership scale from 1-10. The term leader represents a higher level leader on the leadership scale from 1-10.

The higher up the scale the leader is, the higher up the scale his/her followers will be. No matter their level, leaders attract a *"tribe"* or group that chooses to follow because of who the leader is (character), what the leader knows (competency), and where the leader is going (vision).

Within the subgroup of leaders referred to as followers, there is also a range. There are low impact followers and high impact followers.

A low impact follower may choose to follow the leader somewhat blindly and has very little influence left or right with their peers or above with their leader or leaders of others. These followers are doing all they can do to follow effectively.

A high impact follower has influence left and right with their peers and also above with their leader and leaders of others. They have 360° of influence from wherever they are.

> *A low impact follower does*
> *less than is expected alone.*

> *A high impact follower does*
> *more than is expected with others.*

5 Ways High Impact Followers Increase Their Influence

1.   **They add value to the leader.** They make the leader better by looking for ways to help the leader. They do this by doing more than is expected, doing things before they are expected, and doing things better than expected. They also provide valuable unsolicited insight and feedback to the leader.

2.   **They value the leader.** They support the leader. They understand their leader is also their #1 customer. They respect their leader and demonstrate it through their dedication and quality of work.

3.   **They add value to the team.** They make the team better by looking for ways to help others excel. They look for ways to help those needing to be helped. They give credit to the team instead of accepting it for themselves. They develop and nurture sustainable relationships throughout the team.

4.   **They value the team.** They appreciate the differences of each team member. They express gratitude freely and openly. They offer support and share ideas abundantly. They don't focus on *me*, but instead, focus on *we*.

5.   **They invest in personal growth.** This is a trait reserved for the most developed high impact followers. They are well on their way to becoming high impact leaders. They don't wait for anyone to develop them. They develop themselves on purpose for a purpose. As they do, they begin to attract high impact followers.

They will still be capable of following as all great leaders are, but while they are following, others will be following them. When this happens, they have completed the transition from high impact follower to high impact leader. They may not have a formal leadership position yet. But, it's only a matter of time before they will be recognized for their influence and offered one.

"Other people and things can stop you temporarily. YOU are the only one who can do it permanently." ~ Zig Ziglar

20

SEEK FIRST TO UNDERSTAND

YOU WILL ALWAYS LEARN MORE
FROM LISTENING THAN SPEAKING

*"Principles are not invented by us or by society; they are the
laws of the universe that pertain to human relationships
and human organizations. They are part of the human
condition, consciousness, and conscience. To the degree
people recognize and live in harmony with such basic
principles as fairness, equity, justice, integrity, honesty, and
trust, they move toward either survival and stability on the
one hand or disintegration and destruction on the other."*
~ Stephen R. Covey

When you align your values with the principles Covey
described above, amazing things begin to happen in your life at
work and at home. When it comes to influence, one of the best
ways to influence another person is to *first* be influenced by the
other person. That's a choice high impact leaders make.

They let others go first and give their full attention to
understanding them, not agreeing or disagreeing with them,
but understanding them.

*"Authentic listening is not easy. We hear the words, but
rarely do we really slow down to listen and squint with our
ears to hear the emotions, fears, and underlying concerns."*
~ Kevin Cashman

Think about how you feel when your boss listens to you
first. If your boss does his/her best to fully understand your
point of view, what's important to you, and why you feel the
way you do about an issue, are you more or less likely to listen

to their point of view when they start talking? No doubt, you're much more likely to listen to the boss once you feel understood by the boss.

When your boss seeks to first understand you, they are actually being a leader not a boss. That's a good thing!

> *"You can win more friends with your ears than with your mouth. People who feel like they're being listened to feel accepted and appreciated. They feel like they're being taken seriously and what they say really matters."*
> *~ Harvey Mackay*

The reason you're more likely to listen to them better is because you feel whatever they say, they are saying it with a full and complete understanding of your point of view. And, they are. In other words, you will trust their words and opinions more if you feel they have considered your point of view before they share their point of view.

However, if they start out by trying to get you to understand them first, you're most likely focused on wanting to tell them your opinion, or what you think they do or don't know, or what you think they do or don't understand. When this happens, you're not really listening at all. You're just anxiously waiting to reply as soon as they pause to take a breath. I know. I've been there many times.

What do you do if the boss doesn't want to listen first, which means he/she doesn't want your influence at that moment?

> *"Be prepared to listen, and listen to be prepared."*
> *~ Michael F. Sciortino, Sr.*

What do you do? You switch your role and become the leader instead of the follower. Yes, you can do that. Leading is not about having a position. Leading is about increasing your influence.

You don't need a position to be a leader. But, you do need a position to be a boss. To be a leader, all you must do is apply leadership principles. This is why you can lead effectively from the front lines. All you must do to lead is learn leadership principles and start applying them in all of your relationships at work and at home. Then, you are leading.

What would a leader do when their boss doesn't want to listen to them? A leader would immediately seek first to understand the boss. The leader would know the boss would then be more likely to listen to them once they're done.

If you want to be a high impact leader on the front lines, master this leadership principle. *Seek first to understand, then to be understood.*

This is actually Habit 5 from *The 7 Habits of Highly Effective People* written by Stephen R. Covey. Out of the hundreds of books I have read, this remains my all-time favorite. No other book has come close to knocking it out of the top spot on my list. Covey nailed it! If you're enjoying what you're learning in this book, go ahead and prepare to keep growing and get yourself a copy of *The 7 Habits.*

I learned how to transform my life using it as a reference as I've asked you to use my book, relative to learning how to lead from the front lines.

Of course, since I started from where you are now, you also should consider reading my book, *Defining Influence,* which details much of my long journey from front line factory worker to leadership expert, motivational speaker, executive coach/mentor, and author. It also includes a much more in-depth dive into the principles of influence I learned to effectively apply along the way.

If you want to lead from the front lines, *seek first to understand* your peers, your boss, the boss's boss, the engineers, and the other support people. In other words, everybody.

*"Listening requires giving up our favorite human pastime—
involvement in ourselves and our own self-interest.
It's our primary, entirely human focus. And it's where our
motivation to do anything comes from. With this as a base,
can you see what a problem is created when we're asked
to listen to someone else?" ~ Sonya Hamlin*

21

THINK OF YOURSELF LESS

THERE'S A FINE LINE BETWEEN ARROGANCE AND CONFIDENCE; IT'S CALLED HUMILITY

"People with humility don't think less of themselves. They just think about themselves less." ~ Ken Blanchard

I've worked with thousands of front line blue-collar workers across various industries in many different parts of the U.S.A. and Mexico. They are some of the most dedicated, hard-working, and loyal people I've had the privilege of working with and learning from. They also know how to make things happen!

They have taught me a lot, and for that, I'll be forever grateful.

I've always been a seeker of knowledge. When I was on the front lines, I was never happy to just load the machines and push the buttons. I wanted to know why we did things a certain way. I wanted to know how we did it in the past. And most importantly, I wanted to figure out how we could do it better and be more productive in the future. I'm simply curious about everything.

If you're not curious, you need to become curious about being curious. How do you do that? Use a beginner's mindset.

What does it look like to have a beginner's mindset when it comes to curiosity? It looks very much like the little girl who kept asking her mother question after question. Finally the mother cried, *"For heaven's sake, stop asking so many questions. Curiosity killed the cat."*

After two minutes of thinking, the little girl asked, *"So what did the cat want to know?"*

I can relate. Since I'm always interested in learning more, I ask a lot of questions. My favorite questions is: Why? When you ask *"Why?"* your entire life, you get the opportunity to learn more than just the answers to all the questions you're asking. You get to learn about the character of the people providing the answers.

When it comes to *knowing what you're doing* on the front lines, I've discovered there are primarily three groups of people:

1. People who don't want to share any knowledge because they are insecure and feel threatened by others knowing what they know.
2. People who are happy to share their knowledge with you because they want to help you learn. Their focus is on helping you grow and move forward.
3. People who are happy to share their knowledge with you because they want to feel special. Their focus is on appearing to be smarter than you, and anyone else for that matter.

I'll discuss those who don't want to share knowledge in chapter 23. For now, let's focus on those who do.

Group two wants to help because they value helping you and are able to do so because they have the knowledge and experience. The people in this group are sharp and come across as having confidence because they also have humility.

"Humility means knowing and using your strength for the benefit of others, on behalf of a higher purpose. The humble leader is not weak, but strong...is not pre-occupied with self, but with how best to use his or her strengths for the good of others. A humble leader does not think less of himself, but chooses to consider the needs of others in fulfilling a worthy cause. We love to be in the presence of a humble leader because they bring out the very best in us. Their focus is on our purpose, our contribution, and our ability to accomplish all we set out to accomplish." ~ Alan Ross

Group three wants to help because they value appearing smarter than others and are able to do so because they also have the knowledge and experience. The people in this group are sharp too but come across as being arrogant because they don't have humility.

The only difference between the two groups of people with a desire to help is *humility*. Confidence without humility is called *arrogance*. I'm sure you've seen both on the front lines.

Which type of person do you prefer to get your information from? A confident person? Or, an arrogant person? Which person would have more positive influence on the front lines? *Are you arrogant or confident?*

If you truly want to lead from the front lines and be recognized for your leadership ability with or without a position, you *must* be willing to freely and openly share your knowledge with others.

But, when it comes to *"creating your future"* you have a choice to make. Will your future be based on a foundation of arrogance or confidence? It's a *choice* only you can make.

When it comes to leading from the front lines with moral authority, trust is the foundation of influence. If you come across as arrogant, you present a *me* attitude. If you come across as confident, you present a *we* attitude.

People with a *me* attitude create distrust with others and have less influence. People with a *we* attitude build trust with others and have more influence.

Confident people also build trust by telling you they don't know when they don't know because they value *helping* you and realize misleading you doesn't help. But, arrogant people tend to create distrust by pretending to know when they don't, or worse, lie about it because they value *appearing* smart.

"We all know that perfection is a mask. So, we don't trust the people behind know-it-all masks. They're not being honest with us. The people with whom we have the deepest connection are those who acknowledge their weaknesses."
~ Parker Palmer

22

ASK FOR MORE RESPONSIBILITY

WHEN YOU ACCEPT MORE RESPONSIBILITY, YOU WILL GAIN MORE INFLUENCE

"If we embrace the chance of living life to the fullest, then we must be willing to accept responsibility for doing it."
~ Ria Story

The quickest way you build trust from the front lines with your boss is to get results. The easiest way to ensure you don't have a boss looking over your shoulder is to get results. The quickest way to increase your influence with the boss is to get results.

It's probably no surprise most people have learned if they get really great results, they will be asked to do more and be involved in more things. Why? Because they *get results* and bosses depend heavily on the people on the front lines who get the best results. If you were the boss, you would too.

Makes perfect sense to me. They are the ones making things happen!

Far too often, some people attempt to regulate their efforts when they understand how bosses think and what bosses do.

They hold back a little. Their goal is to do what *they* consider to be a good job, not too far ahead of others and not too far behind others. Nice and smooth right down the middle, so they can feel secure about maintaining a steady income, feel good about giving an honest day's work for an honest day's pay, and avoid being asked to do more than what they already have to do.

They are not bad people. But, they also are not exceptional people. They are average people doing what average people do, a good job.

Doing a good job is not a bad thing,
but doing a great job is an exceptional thing.

When it comes to leading from the front lines, it's all about increasing your influence with the high impact leaders in the organization. You don't do that by being an average team member, you do that by being an exceptional team member.

I'm assuming since you're still reading this book, I've got your attention. You're interested. Or at least, you're still curious.

What I know about you is you are already exceptional or you're on the verge of making some changes and will soon become exceptional. Either way, I'm proud of you for sticking with me, and I'm excited about the future you are choosing.

If you want to be a game changer, get noticed, and make a high impact, average people make it easy for you to shine.

I learned how to become exceptional early in my career when I noticed how those around me could do more but wouldn't. I've been doing it relentlessly my entire career. It's very simple and easy to do. Anyone with ambition to move beyond average can get started the next time they go to work.

It's another one of those common sense things too. It makes perfect sense. Yet, few people do it because it takes uncommon sense to act.

Most of the time it's not easy to get pay increases or promotions. There is only so much in the pot and only so many positions to be filled. If you want to climb the *"corporate ladder"* and the *"corporate pay scale"* you must make what I'm about to share a habit for the rest of your career. It will make you an exceptional team member in the eyes of high impact leaders faster than anything else.

Don't ask for a raise; ask for more responsibility.

I learned early in my career most people complain about

their pay. They don't feel like they are paid enough. And as a result, they don't give their all on the job. They let their feelings get in the way. They have the mindset of *"If they will pay me more, I will do more."* So, their focus is on getting a raise instead of doing a better job.

When you start a new job at a new company, you don't show up on the first day and receive two weeks of pay. That doesn't happen. You must work two weeks first. Then, you get paid for two weeks. That's a principle. We must do the work before we get paid for doing it.

That's why asking for more responsibility instead of a raise is such a powerful way to leverage your influence. Ask to be on improvement teams. Ask to be on special projects. Ask what you can do to help. Get involved. Volunteer for special events.

Everyone appreciates someone sincerely wanting to help.

Or, don't ask. Just do. Do what you know needs to be done but isn't getting done whether it's your responsibility or not. Make it your responsibility. Make it happen. This is not a hard thing to do. If you have the time and the ability, do it.

The best businesses over deliver right? Remember, you're working for yourself. So, over deliver to improve your *word of mouth* advertisement. People will notice. You will build new relationships and gain influence in new areas with new people.

Don't worry about the average people giving you a hard time. Trust me. They will. I can't tell you how many times I heard *"There goes a shooting star."* or *"There you go sucking up again."* Some were much worse. I won't share them here.

What you need to know is average people *aren't willing* to do what exceptional people *are willing* to do. They say, *"You're making us look bad."* That's one of the ways they try to pull you back down to their level. It's tough when they're in the group of five people you hang around the most. If someone doesn't want you to do well, are they for you or against you?

Are you living your life by default or by design?

23

THERE IS ENOUGH FOR EVERYONE

HELPING OTHERS SUCCEED
ENSURES YOU WILL SUCCEED

"Coming together is a beginning. Keeping together is progress. Working together is success." ~ Henry Ford

In chapter 21, I mentioned there are *"People who don't want to share any knowledge because they are insecure and feel threatened by others knowing what they know."*

Insecure people have what's called a *scarcity* mindset. They believe there is only so much of a given thing *"out there,"* and everything is limited. They think like this: If you get a raise, I won't. If you get a promotion, I won't. If you get credit for doing something, I won't. If you get noticed, I won't.

Scarcity minded people also tend to blame others when they don't get what they want. I didn't get a raise because someone else got a raise. I didn't get promoted because someone else got promoted. I didn't get credit because someone else got credit. I didn't get noticed because someone else got noticed. And on, and on…

Think back to some of the previous chapters. Scarcity minded people don't look in the mirror. They look out the window. They don't take responsibility. They don't pause and respond based on values in alignment with natural laws and principles. They react based on feelings. They are focused on me, not we. I hope by now you are beginning to see how all of these chapters tie together.

There is a *synergy* created when they are all used together. Synergy means the whole is greater than the sum of the parts. Some in my training sessions struggle to understand the concept of synergy. Synergy simply means there is an unseen value when considering the relationship between two or more things, like all of the principles of influence (leadership) I'm sharing. Or, the parts of a car.

Imagine you have two garages with the exact same brand new car, but there's a catch. One garage has a completely assembled car ready to drive. The other garage has a completely disassembled car, a pile of all the parts it takes to make the complete car but not a single part is connected to another. Which car is more valuable to you? If the selling price was the same, which would you buy? How much more would you pay for the assembled car compared to the disassembled car?

Obviously, everyone would value the assembled car more. Why? Because there are thousands of valuable relationships, a synergy, between all of the connected parts allowing the car to function which creates a greater value and serves a higher purpose. The disassembled car has none of those relationships.

You could also remove some of the parts from the assembled car, and it may still function without much of an impact on the value. But, you could also remove some very critical parts. If only one of those parts were removed, the car wouldn't function at all and would have a greatly reduced value.

That's a simple example to help you see synergy in action. The same thing is at play with all of the leadership (influence) principles I'm sharing with you throughout this book. They all impact your influence to some degree. Some more than others.

Choosing scarcity would be like having a perfectly functioning car but trying to drive it around while keeping your foot pressed firmly on the brake the entire time. That wouldn't make a lot of sense right? Neither does choosing scarcity in an abundant world.

Average people have a scarcity mindset. They're not bad people because of it. But I can tell you this, they are not *exceptional* people because of it. If you want to be exceptional, you must get a lot of the things I mention in this book right consistently and over a long period of time. They must become habits.

The good news is having a scarcity mindset is a choice. A choice to believe what insecure, average people believe and to do what they do because of it. If you can choose to have a scarcity mindset, you can also choose not to have a scarcity mindset. You could choose an abundance mindset instead.

Exceptional, secure people have an *abundance* mindset. They believe there is enough of everything for everyone. They think like this: If you can get a raise, I can get a raise too. If you can get a promotion, I can get a promotion too. If you can get credit, I can get credit too. If you can get noticed, I can get noticed too.

> *"Abundance is not something we acquire.*
> *It is something we tune into." ~ Wayne Dyer*

When you choose abundance, you don't hoard knowledge. You share it openly and freely. You want to help others get ahead because you know helping others helps you. Common sense again.

Assume you're the boss and can promote one of two people. Everything is equal but one thing. One doesn't share knowledge and doesn't want to help others succeed. One shares knowledge intentionally to help others succeed. The one sharing with abundance gets promoted. Look at it from a different angle. There has been a drop in customer orders. Unfortunately, you must let one go. Which one loses their job? Obviously, the knowledge hoarder with scarcity.

Interestingly, those hoarding knowledge because of scarcity believe knowing more and sharing less makes them more valuable and more secure. That's because they're insecure. Those with an abundance mindset are free to share their knowledge because they are secure and know their true value.

> *"Nothing can stop the man with the right mental attitude*
> *from achieving his goals; nothing on earth can help the*
> *man with the wrong mental attitude." ~ Thomas Jefferson*

24

BE THE FIRST TO HELP

EVERYONE REMEMBERS THE FIRST TO HELP; FEW REMEMBER THE SECOND

"Leaders are not always the first to see the need for change, but they are the first to act. And once they move away from the pack, they are positioned to lead."
~ Andy Stanley

Helping others helps us. Not sometime, every time.

There's actually a chemical response that naturally occurs in our body which causes us to feel good when we help someone. It also causes us to feel good when someone helps us. It's really interesting because it also happens to us when we see someone helping another person, even when we are not involved.

People may not always remember what you said or what you did, but they will always remember how you made them feel. When they feel good because of you, your influence goes up. When they feel bad because of you, your influence goes down.

Greg Williams, 4-time National Champion Head Coach of the Auburn University Equestrian Team, is a client and friend of mine. I had the privilege of conducting leadership development sessions with him and his coaching staff for several years. The first thing I ever noticed about Greg that really stood out to me was that he was always the first to help.

Not sometimes, all the time. Not just at work, but at home and everywhere in between too. It's in his DNA.

I had read about this principle and began to apply it in my life before I met Greg. It doesn't come naturally to me. It's not that I don't want to help. I simply must work harder at paying more attention to others, so I'll know when they need help. It comes naturally to Greg without any effort.

I had never really seen it in action by someone who is a natural helper (a servant leader). He's got a sixth sense about knowing when someone needs assistance, or better yet, should be given assistance whether they need it or not. I don't mean just the big things. He does those too. I mean the little things. He models this principle 24/7/365. It's in his heart to help others. As a result, he is always the first to help.

With people, the little things are the big things.

Whether it's getting ahead of someone to open a door, walking someone to their car to help them carry a load, picking up something someone has just dropped, walking someone to their car in the rain holding an umbrella, it gets noticed.

There are endless ways to help others on the front lines. You simply must be willing to do it because it's the right thing to do.

It took me years of applying the principles I'm sharing in this book before I was able to work my way off of the front lines and into upper management before eventually starting my own business. I never have stopped supporting those on the front lines however. The evidence is right here on these pages. I have never forgotten you, and I never will. You and the potential within you matter to me. This book is a small effort to *be the first to help* you unleash your potential. I hope to help many people I will most likely never meet.

You can take action from wherever you are. Get started. Help others with no expectations of getting help in return, and you'll be amazed at how much influence you will gain and how good you will feel. One of the best ways to turn a bad day into a good day is to find someone needing help and help them.

A few examples from the front lines come to mind. In the past, I operated a large twin spindle lathe. During the machining process, a lot of metal chips were created. They went out the backside of the machine on a conveyor. There were three of those machines in a row. Each had an operator like me. I don't remember who started it, but I do remember it happening regularly. Whenever one of us would go behind our machine to pull out the chips into the scrap bin, we would also take care of the others too. It was just something we did to help. We were a team even though it wasn't official.

However, when I worked a different shift, this wasn't common practice with those individuals. Everyone took care of their own chips and went back to work. All it took was to do it for the others a few times. Then, they all started doing it for each other too. *Leadership is influence.*

Leadership is more caught than taught.

I also remember another time after I had climbed my way into upper management, only one position from the top. I was walking through the plant, and someone stopped me and asked me for a broom. I was always wearing blue jeans and a t-shirt with a pair of gloves in my back pocket in case I needed to help someone while I was on the plant floor.

I couldn't believe she was asking me for a broom. Not because I was too good to be asked, but because there were officially several leaders between her and me. Why hadn't they helped I wondered? How long had she needed a broom? How hard could it be to get someone to get you a broom?

After talking with her, I found out she had asked her team leader and supervisor several times over the past few weeks without any luck. She said she decided to ask me because she knew I would get it. Her words made me feel good. I didn't do anything else until I had delivered her broom. I didn't continue on with my task, I was afraid I might forget and be just like the others. I didn't want to be known for letting people down.

Often, all you must do to help is make someone smile.

"By accident of fortune one may be a leader for a time, but by helping others succeed one will be a leader forever."
~ Chinese Proverb

25

DO MORE THAN EXPECTED

DOING MORE INCREASES YOUR INFLUENCE; DOING LESS DECREASES YOUR INFLUENCE

"Never mistake effort and intentions for results."
~ Dick Vermeil

The rest of this book is about accepting responsibility at a higher level. You do that by embracing the challenge of becoming exceptional on the front lines and/or by moving beyond the front lines if that's the future you want to create for yourself. If you turn the principles in this book into habits, your options will be unlimited.

Too many people on the front lines wait to be told what to do while often complaining about not liking to be told what to do. They don't feel responsible for deciding what to do next. You'll hear things like: *"That's above my pay grade."* Or, *"They don't pay me to think."*

I actually heard that last one every day from one of my team leaders when I was on the front lines. That was his response whenever any of us asked him a question he didn't know the answer to. He wasn't a bad guy, but he was a long way from being an exceptional guy. We either figured it out ourselves, went above his head at the first opportunity, or never got an answer.

The first level of responsibility above waiting to be told is to ask what to do next when you've completed a task or can no longer do what the boss thinks you are doing. When you ask, you have taken on a *very small* amount of responsibility to move beyond standing around waiting, which doesn't increase your influence with any high impact leaders, to begin looking for something to do, which does increase your influence with those expecting you to be doing something to help the team accomplish the mission.

When you *ask*, all you *must* do is *ask*. The boss still has to do all the thinking and may not have nearly as much information about what's going in your area as you do. So, he/she will often have to get back with you while they go find out what's going on.

An average person doesn't mind waiting. I've heard them say many times, *"I don't mind waiting. I get paid the same either way."* They don't have a clue what the *word of mouth* advertisement they are spreading out of their own mouth is doing to *their* business (their ability to get raises, recognition, and promotions).

An exceptional person doesn't like to wait. They are not there to *"just get paid."* They are there to make an impact and be seen as valuable by anyone watching them. We don't like to be seen standing around because we know that's bad for *our* business, no matter if we're getting paid the same or not.

If you truly want to step up to the plate, accept more responsibility, and lead from the front lines, move beyond asking what to do next and *start recommending* what you should do next when you have the opportunity.

When you do, everything changes because you have started thinking. But, what you're actually doing during the process is learning, demonstrating to the boss you can think, revealing to the boss how you think, and playing a bigger role in deciding what you may actually be doing next.

There's a good chance what you recommend may not be what the boss wants you to do. That's okay. He/she will have a lot of information about the bigger picture you may not have. If the boss wants you to do something else, there's a good chance they will still appreciate your effort to help them.

They will also probably feel obligated to explain to you why they want you to do something else which will allow you to begin learning more about the big picture. As you begin to learn more about the big picture, your recommendations will get better. Once the boss sees you are a thinker and are always recommending a course of action, he/she will start sharing more information with you, so you can make better recommendations. When this happens, you are becoming more valuable to the boss and the company.

There's no need to share all of that information with you when all you do is wait to be told what to do or ask what to do. That just slows down the boss. But, when you're recommending, the boss can feel and sense you're trying to help them. Therefore, they start helping you help them.

You may recommend the right things to the boss from the start, or it may take a while before you learn how the boss thinks and what he/she expects.

Trust me. When you're recommending the right things, the boss will notice and know they can depend on you. Slowly, but in some cases quickly, you will be given more responsibility. Don't worry about getting paid more because you have more responsibility. Just do it.

When the time is right, the experience you gain by stepping up will get you a raise, a promotion, or often both. This is why you intentionally focus on becoming more valuable, not more successful. *Leaders are learners.* You may be ridiculed by those around you. If you plan to start applying what I'm teaching you, prepare for it. It comes with choosing to lead.

If you were the boss, who would you value more. Someone waiting to be told what to do? Someone asking what to do? Or, someone that considers the situation, thinks about the mission and what you would want done, and recommends a course of action? As you know, the answer is common sense.

If you really want to make a high impact as a front line leader, start recommending opportunities for improvements.

*"Start doing what is necessary; then, do what is possible;
and suddenly you are doing the impossible."
~ St. Francis of Assisi*

26

DO IT SOONER THAN EXPECTED

DOING IT SOONER INCREASES YOUR INFLUENCE; DOING IT LATER DECREASES YOUR INFLUENCE

"The wise does at once what the fool does at last."
~ Jewish Proverb

The front lines in most organizations are extremely busy with constant changes of some type taking place for various reasons and the pressure to produce is usually coming from multiple angles. The blue-collar workers on the front lines are a special breed. They always find a way to make it happen.

Making it happen is great, but making it happen sooner than expected can pay huge in the influence department. Why? Because you're building trust.

When you choose to do things sooner rather than later, you are building a strong foundational layer of *trust* that will benefit you today and into the future as you are asked to do bigger and better things. Trust is the foundation of influence.

"The beauty of trust is that it erases worry and frees you to get on with other matters. Trust means confidence."
~ Stephen M. R. Covey

When you are doing things sooner than expected, the boss has more confidence in you. He/she will begin to go to you first. Yes, you will get more responsibility and be expected to do more. We've covered that already. That's a good thing.

If you do things later than expected, you will create distrust. The boss will lose confidence and starting depending on someone else. In other words, you are choosing to let the train pass you buy. You either get on the train and go for a ride, or stand alongside the tracks while it passes you by.

"Even if you are on the right track,
you'll get run over if you just sit there." ~ Will Rogers

Without trust, you will only have influence if you have a title or a position with formal authority. You're the boss, or mom, or dad in a position where others *"have"* to follow you. Or, you physically or mentally manipulate and influence others through fear and intimidation. Both of these are the lowest levels of influence and are weak at best. None build trust. And, if the formal authority was taken away. No one would follow.

The only influence that truly has any meaningful value is based on moral authority. Every principle I'm teaching you in this book, if applied, will allow you to build trust. If you do nothing or the opposite of the principle, you create distrust.

When you choose to influence others with moral authority, position or title doesn't matter. Fear and intimidation doesn't exist. Others *"want"* to follow you because of who you are. Influence is based on trust that has been earned primarily through personal character development. You influence others because they allow you to because they respect you for who you are. No title or position is required. Anyone at any level can lead this way.

The front line is the perfect place to build trust and gain influence using the principle of *doing it sooner than expected* because you don't need a position. All you need is the desire to excel, to give the extra effort required, and to understand the impact it will have on your relationship with the boss. Don't forget, the boss is your #1 customer.

Don't miss the point here. You don't only want to build trust with the boss. You want to build trust and influence with as many people as possible. You may need their help one day.

Consider the previous story I shared about the broom. I was an upper level leader, and the person needing the broom was on the front lines. That didn't matter. She had been waiting for a broom for several weeks. The other leaders between us hadn't delivered on their promise. They were obviously in the *later than expected* category creating distrust on the front lines with their own team members.

However, I responded to the front line worker just as I would have done for my boss. For me, there was no difference. I see them both as people, unrelated to their positions. I made it happen. She had the broom as soon as I could locate one. And, I delivered it *sooner than expected.*

If I had to guess, I bet I got some good *word of mouth* advertising as a result. I'm sure someone heard about my quick response and the lack of response from the others. My influence increased. Their influence decreased.

When someone doesn't trust you, it's not their fault. It's your fault. You can't make someone trust you. You can only make choices that make you trustworthy. Then, others can choose to trust or distrust you based on your choices.

With trust, we always know.
Without trust, we never know.

With trust, everything is possible.
Without trust, everything is questioned.

With trust, things happen fast.
Without trust, things happen slowly, if at all.

With trust, relationships strengthen.
Without trust, relationships weaken.

Who do you need to build trust with? What do you need to do differently? What would stop you from doing it? Don't buy into your excuses. Make it happen! Your future depends on it.

"The successful person has the habit of doing the things
failures don't like to do." ~ E. M. Gray

27

DO IT BETTER THAN EXPECTED

DOING IT BETTER INCREASES YOUR INFLUENCE; DOING IT WORSE DECREASES YOUR INFLUENCE

"When you do the common things in life in an uncommon way, you will command the attention of the world."
~ *George Washington Carver*

When you pay attention to the details and go above and beyond expectations, people pay attention to you.

The pride you take in your work shows. It builds trust and influence because you are saying through your actions, *"What I'm doing matters to me."* It's not about what you're being paid to do the work. It is based on the fact *you* are doing it.

It's also not tied to how you're treated. Value driven people *do it better than expected* because they *value* doing a better job than expected. They understand they are working for themselves. It's about improving their reputation and growing their influence.

Value driven people understand this principle. They know the quality of their work reflects the quality of their character. And for them, character always counts.

If you want to do it better than expected on the front lines, do two things: 1) Focus on developing yourself. 2) Focus on improving the processes where you work.

Basically, make yourself better and make your job better. I've just described the perfect, *High Impact* front line leader.

You can really gain tremendous synergy by blending doing more than expected with doing it sooner and better than expected. The result is proactive process improvement. That's a big deal on the front lines. All companies expect this from those on the front lines, but few actually get it. There are not enough exceptional people to make this common. It is uncommon because exceptional people are uncommon.

I've been trying to *do it better than expected* my entire career. I've written this book to help you do it better than expected.

I have the perfect example to share with you from my days on the front lines. In 1998, I applied for an open position in a manufacturing cell on the day shift. I had been on the night shift for 10 years and was anxious to start sleeping at night instead of working at night.

This work cell had only been in place for a year. It was not producing at the expected rate. The guy who had been running it from the beginning had been complaining it would never work since day one. Many mornings after my shift, I would see him as he was coming in to work. All I heard for an entire year was moaning, groaning, and whining. Without much support, the other two shifts simply did their best to be productive.

All of the engineering, supervisors, upper level managers, etc. were on the day shift. So, they were all involved non-stop trying to increase the output without much luck. I was actually looking forward to joining the effort.

I had always liked a challenge and had been waiting to get on day shift where all of the support people were. I knew they had knowledge, and I would be able to learn a lot from all of them. This was the perfect opportunity since the spot light was already shining bright right where I would be standing, in the middle of the worst performing cell in the plant. What better place to show your best than in the place considered the worst?

I thought it would be easy to stand out. I immediately started applying the many principles I've shared with you. I hadn't read a single leadership book. But, I had slowly, over time, learned what worked and what didn't. I was on a mission.

This cell had a twin spindle lathe, a gear shaper, and a vertical milling center. There was a lot going on for one person along with all of the various quality inspections. In the past, each machine had stood alone, each with an operator. So, there used to be three people operating all of these machines with each person also conducting their individual inspections.

This was one reason the old-timer was frustrated. He was against the cellular layout design from the start. He said it was too much for one man. I just thought it was too much for *that* man. Time would tell. It was about to be my turn to see what I could make happen.

I used a *do it better than expected* approach. I didn't just run the machines, do what the support people said do, and go home. I asked for responsibility. I stepped up and joined their team by getting much more involved than the other guy had. He wasn't a bad guy. He just wasn't an *exceptional* guy.

I started a spreadsheet and started collecting cycle times on every part on every machine, so I would know where the bottle neck (the slowest cycle time) was each time I would run a different part. I kept busy all day long trying to figure out how to make the slowest machine cycle faster (better). I also did the same thing relative to changeover when all the machines would have to be retooled for different sizes and types of parts.

I loved every minute of it. After only six months of *recommending* program changes, I had learned to read and edit all of the programs for all of the machines. I was becoming more valuable but not *yet* getting paid more. I had helped the support team double the output of the cell across all shifts, the equivalent of adding an additional new cell and three more operators based on the old output. We had it humming!

As a result of my *doing more, sooner, and better than expected*, I was later offered a CNC programming position which was responsible for programming nearly 70 CNC machines. I accepted the promotion, along with a big pay raise, and began supporting the front lines instead of working on the front lines.

I had simply made a choice to *do it better than expected.*

"Don't measure yourself by what you have accomplished,
but rather by what you should have accomplished
with your ability." ~ John Wooden

28

STRETCH YOURSELF INTENTIONALLY

ALL OF YOUR GROWTH HAPPENS
OUTSIDE YOUR COMFORT ZONE

*"If you work hard on your job you can make a living, but if
you work hard on yourself you can make a fortune."*
~ Jim Rohn

I've always been a value driven person. I've had great
bosses and not so great bosses, but my production numbers
were always high because I was working for me not them.

I never needed a boss to stretch me or challenge me
because I was always stretching myself and asking the boss for
more responsibility to keep myself growing. Actually, they
couldn't keep up with my requests to do more and learn more.

My biggest challenge at work was dealing with boredom
that would set in after I had been doing the same thing for too
long. I was usually able to change jobs every year or two, but
much more than a year on a job, and I was bored. However, I
did use my time wisely. I actually read all of the machine
manuals on any of the equipment I was operating at the time.

I've always been comfortable being uncomfortable which
means I embrace change and challenge. The more you embrace
change and challenge, the more valuable you will become to
others. Why? Because that's when all of your learning and
personal growth happens. That's where you gain new *experience.*

I remember when I was offered the CNC programming
position. There were a lot of angry people. That was a highly
sought after position that rarely had an opening. There were
people with many more years of service who applied for the
job, but it was offered to me.

Too often, people on the front lines get upset when someone with fewer years of service passes by them. In my case, I had been moving constantly during the 10 years I had been there. I had been a saw operator, a drill operator, a small cell operator, a broach/drill/tap operator, a setup technician (where I learned to operate and setup nearly all of the 70 machines in the plant), a quality technician, and lastly a large cell operator where I helped double the output in six months.

I actually had 10 years of experience. Most of the people who applied for the programming job had been on the same job for years, stuck in their comfort zone. Instead of having 10 years of experience, they actually had one year of experience on the same job repeated many times.

Most had learned very little about programming. They were waiting until they got the programmer's job to learn how to do that. They could only operate and setup a few machines because when the setup technician job was created on the night shift, none of them wanted to stretch themselves and get out of their comfort zone (the day shift). That's the only reason I was able to get the job at that time. None of them wanted it, and I was glad they didn't because I did.

I was choosing to be stretched like never before learning to operate all of those machines. Some were similar, but most were completely different. I was trained non-stop to operate the various machines by many different operators for nearly two years straight. I built a lot of relationships which allowed me to increase my influence (leadership) across the entire plant.

You can choose your actions but not the consequences that flow from those actions. What should you be doing at work to stretch yourself? What should you be doing at home to stretch yourself relative to making yourself more valuable at work?

Growing yourself after hours, at home, is where you can get ahead quickly compared to those who only grow at work. However, in my early years, it never occurred to me that I should be stretching myself when I wasn't at work.

Choosing to stretch yourself isn't about how smart you are. It's about how secure you are.

"No amount of personal competency can compensate for personal insecurity." ~ Wayne Smith

You need to stretch yourself for yourself. If you want to grow your business (YOU), there's only one way. You've got to move beyond your comfort zone. All of your growth happens outside your comfort zone. That's why it's uncomfortable. If you're comfortable, you're not growing. You're coasting. Growth doesn't just happen. You must make it happen.

If you're waiting on the company to stretch you, or worse, trying to avoid being stretched by the company, you're growing far too slowly or, most likely, not at all. When you start turning down offers that will stretch you, it's only a matter of time before you will be passed up by those who are accepting those offers of change and challenge.

When there are openings in the company, I can tell you who will get the job every time. The person with the most influence based on what the boss values in relation to the position. I can promise you it will always be the person he/she *trusts* to do the best job. Trust is the foundation of influence.

Some will say it's luck. But, luck is where preparation intersects opportunity. If you want to be lucky when new jobs come open, be prepared before they come open. How do you do that? You may study at home by reading related books or watching videos on the internet. You may volunteer to work in other areas even if it's overtime. The people who get promoted are those most prepared when the opportunity comes.

What you've already done up to this moment has allowed you to be where you are today, doing what you're doing today. If you want to make a bigger impact, you've got to make a bigger impact on yourself first. If you don't know where you want to be in five years, you're already there. Think about that.

"When we are faced with change, we either step forward into growth or we step backward into safety."
~ Abraham Maslow

29

DEVELOP YOURSELF INTENTIONALLY

IF YOU WON'T INVEST IN YOURSELF, WHY SHOULD ANYONE ELSE?

"Accidental growth vs. intentional growth is about as effective as accidental exercise compared to intentional exercise....not even close. And the results....not even close."
~ Mack Story

Once you begin to stretch yourself, you're perfectly positioned to develop yourself. It took me many years to figure out I, not someone else or my company, was responsible for developing me.

If you don't know where you want to be in five years, you're already there. What does that mean exactly? It means until you develop a plan and act on that plan, you will be exactly where you are today with the exception of accidental, incremental growth along the way.

Think back to my story of starting college because the engineer shared his belief in me when I was 25 years old. Well, up to that point I didn't have a plan, and I had been doing the same entry-level job for the last six years, operating machines.

Once I developed a plan to go to college, I took action. A lot started to happen after that. I started going to college to get my two year degree. Then, I went back to get my four year degree. Then, I started reading process improvements books. Then, I started reading leadership books every day. Soon after I started truly investing in myself, new doors started opening, doors I hadn't even considered walking through in the past.

There are so many opportunities waiting for you *after* you have prepared for them, but *not before*. When high impact leaders in your organization see you are engaged and moving yourself forward, they will take notice. If you've become an exceptional front line leader, they will know you are on a mission to move up or out. They will not want you to move out, so they'll start figuring out new ways to engage and use you. You won't know this is happening until the time is right.

Don't worry about what's going to happen, where it's going to happen, or when it's going to happen. All you need to do is *focus on what you want to happen*. Then, get to work intentionally preparing yourself to make it happen.

As an example, let's assume you're on the front lines making it happen and you're an exceptional team member achieving amazing results in your *comfort zone* with the desire to work your way into some other roles in the company. There's a really strong chance you will need computer skills once you move away from the front lines.

If you don't have computer skills, you won't be prepared for an opportunity that requires them. In other words, you'll be out of *luck*. You will most likely get passed up by someone potentially with less experience in the company but more experience with computers.

Someone in this situation who continues to choose accidental growth will only gain additional computer skills when they are *required to*. If they aren't required to, they won't ever develop them. They will simply *hope* to get a job where they can be trained on a computer. That's not leading from the front lines. That's following from a distance while trying to keep up and hoping for something better one day.

Hope is not a strategy.
However, hope is needed to develop a strategy.

Without hope, there will be no sacrifice. If you don't believe strongly enough in yourself and your vision for the future, you will not have the strength or desire to make the sacrifices needed to transform your vision into your reality. You will remain exactly where you're supposed to be based on your choices and the sacrifices you *are willing* to make. If you want to move closer to your vision, you must make different choices and additional sacrifices. *Hope won't make it happen.*

> *Sacrifice is giving up something of lesser value now for something of greater value later.*

Someone who chooses intentional growth relative to learning computer skills will take action on their own. They may buy a computer and take online courses. They may go to the library where they can do it for free. They may enroll in community courses or even a community college to get a certificate or degree. There are many things they can do.

The one thing they won't do is make excuses for why they can't do it. *Whenever you place the cause of one of your actions outside of yourself, it's an excuse, not a reason.*

> *"Do your excuses serve your dream?"* ~ Scott M. Fay

There's something I learned from my mentor, John Maxwell, called *The Rule of 5*. I use it to grow every day. You can too.

The Rule of 5 means you determine the *most important* thing you want to accomplish intentionally. Next, identify the 5 most important things you must do *every day* to reach the goal. Then, do them *every day* until the goal is met. Not all day, but do some amount of each, no matter how small of an amount, *every day*. Modify your list if necessary, but stay focused on it.

You should do these 5 things *daily*, most likely *after* work, until you reach your goal. Then, develop a new goal and repeat. It's not about making a list. It's about taking action.

Here is my current *Rule of 5* list: 1) Read leadership content 2) Collect and file leadership quotes 3) Write about leadership 4) Connect with people that value leadership 5) Teach people leadership. I've been doing these 5 things daily for years.

> *"Today I will do what others won't, so tomorrow I can do what others can't."* ~ Jerry Rice

30

YOU MUST BET ON YOURSELF

IF YOU WON'T BET ON YOURSELF, WHY SHOULD ANYONE ELSE?

"Living intentionally leads to amazing results. Living accidentally leads to depressing disappointments. A better tomorrow won't just happen. You must be intentional and make it happen." ~ Mack Story

As you grow and develop, new opportunities *will* appear. You *will* develop new relationships along the way that *will* lead to many of those opportunities. People *will* take notice. Discussions about your future *will* happen without your knowledge in many different areas. People who have never talked to you *will* begin talking to you. A lot *will* happen.

Don't give up! Keep hammering away. It may seem like nothing is happening. Real growth takes some time. There are no shortcuts. *If you pay the price, you will reap the reward.* That's another natural law. Trust me. It *will* happen.

I know. I have lived what I've taught you on these pages. I'm not telling you what I've learned from nearly 30 years of research. I'm telling you what I've learned from nearly 30 years of application and transformation. *Nearly 30 years of action!*

Not 30 minutes. Not 30 days. Not 30 months. 30 YEARS!

Everything you've learned so far, if applied, is enough to separate you from the crowd in a relatively short period of time. What you do after that is up to you because as I've shared many times already, you will have many more options.

If you keep repeating the cycle, it will keep happening. As long as you're willing to continue paying the price, you will continue creating more options and building more relationships.

I encourage you to be a river, not a reservoir.

What I mean is don't hoard the knowledge. Let it flow through you and into others, even if your goal it to separate yourself from the crowd. High impact leaders always bring others with them. That's my goal with you right now. I wrote this book because I want to bring you with me.

I believe in you. But, the key is this: you must believe in yourself. As you grow and learn, *you must be willing to bet on yourself.* You will have to step out on a limb and experiment. When you do, don't be afraid to fail. That's how you learn.

As long as you don't quit, you cannot fail. Failing is only failing if you quit trying to learn how to succeed.
If you keep trying, failing is really learning.

Did you fail to walk or did you learn to walk? You learned without knowing how and no one taught you. Your parents didn't teach you. They may have helped you and supported you, but you learned all by yourself. No one can teach you to balance yourself. That has to happen on the inside.

You also didn't learn to walk the first time you tried. You actually failed at learning to walk hundreds, if not thousands of times, but eventually you figured out what to do by learning what not to do. Learning to lead (influence) from the front lines may be the same way for you. Don't give up. Keep trying.

If you're like the rest of us,
there's a lot that's got to happen to you on the inside
before it can happen for you on the outside.

My biggest challenge along the way hasn't been others, although some made it tough on me at times. My biggest challenge has been ME. *I work on ME every day.* Remember, every challenge is an opportunity for growth whether it comes from the inside or the outside.

If this is your first leadership book, you may not realize what has just happened. You have already separated yourself from the great mass of people who have never read a leadership book. *I'm proud of you too!* The majority of people with or without a leadership title have never read a leadership book. You also now have a greater responsibility to help grow and develop others at work and at home. Make it happen!

It's time to place your bet! My money is on you!

> *"To grow, you must be willing to let your present and future be totally unlike your past. Your history is not your destiny."* ~ Alan Cohen

As I mentioned early on, **IF YOU GAINED VALUE FROM THIS BOOK, DO NOT GIVE IT AWAY.** I do encourage you to be intentional as a front line leader. You should encourage others to read it too. If you really want to show someone you believe in them, buy them a copy. Write them a personal note in the front and give it to them as a gift.

Don't hesitate to tell your boss and other managers what you've learned. You should do that because it *will* increase your influence with them. *Buy them a copy or encourage them to buy one for themselves and others at your company.*

I support many companies with billions of dollars in sales each year and operations all over the world and have coached and mentored leaders at all levels. I know anyone at any level in any industry can learn something valuable from this book because it's filled with timeless principles that apply to anyone that values positive influence and wants to help others be better people. *Leaders invest in the development of other people.*

I welcome hearing how this book has influenced the way you think, your life on the front lines, or the results you have achieved because of what you've learned in it. Please feel free to share your thoughts with me by email at:

mack@mackstory.com

To learn more about my books, audiobooks, and podcasts, etc., please visit: BlueCollarLeadership.com

ABOUT THE AUTHOR

Mack's story is an amazing journey of personal and professional growth. He married Ria in 2001. He has one son, Eric, born in 1991.

After graduating high school in 1987, Mack joined the United States Marine Corps Reserve as an 0311 infantryman. Soon after, he began his 20 plus year manufacturing career. Graduating with highest honors, he earned an Executive Bachelor of Business Administration degree from Faulkner University.

Mack began his career in manufacturing in 1988 on the front lines of a large production machine shop. He eventually grew himself into upper management and found his niche in lean manufacturing and along with it, developed his passion for leadership. In 2008, he launched his own Lean Manufacturing and Leadership Development firm.

From 2005-2012, Mack led leaders and their cross-functional teams through more than 11,000 hours of process improvement, organizational change, and cultural transformation. Ria joined Mack full-time in late 2013.

In 2013, they worked with John C. Maxwell as part of an international training event focused on the Cultural Transformation in Guatemala where over 20,000 leaders were trained. They also shared the stage with internationally recognized motivational speaker Les Brown in 2014.

Mack and Ria have published 30+ books on personal growth and leadership development. In 2018, they were invited to speak at Yale University's School of Management. They also had over 80,000 international followers at the end of 2019 on LinkedIn where they provide daily motivational, inspirational, and leadership content to people around the world.

Mack and Ria inspire people everywhere through their example of achievement, growth, and personal development.

Clients: ATD (Association for Talent Development), Auburn University, Chevron, Chick-fil-A, Kimberly Clark, Koch Industries, Southern Company, and the U.S. Military.

WHAT WE OFFER:

- ✓ Keynote Speaking: Conferences, Seminars, Onsite
- ✓ Workshops: Onsite/Offsite Half/Full/Multi Day
- ✓ Leadership Development Support: Leadership, Teamwork, Personal Growth, Organizational Change, Planning, Executing, Trust, Cultural Transformation, Communication, Time Management, Selling with Character, Resilience, & Relationship Building
- ✓ Blue-Collar Leadership® Development
- ✓ Corporate Retreats
- ✓ Women's Retreat (with Ria Story)
- ✓ Limited one-on-one coaching/mentoring
- ✓ On-site Lean Leadership Certification
- ✓ Lean Leader Leadership Development
- ✓ Become licensed to teach our content

FOR MORE INFORMATION PLEASE VISIT:

BlueCollarLeadership.com
RiaStory.com
TopStoryLeadership.com

FOLLOW US ON SOCIAL MEDIA:

LinkedIn.com/in/MackStory
Facebook.com/Mack.Story

LinkedIn.com/in/RiaStory
Facebook.com/Ria.Story

LISTEN/SUBSCRIBE TO OUR PODCASTS AT:

TopStoryLeadership.com/podcast

Excerpt from

Defining Influence:
Increasing Your Influence Increases Your Options

In *Defining Influence*, I outline the foundational leadership principles and lessons we must learn in order to develop our character in a way that allows us to increase our influence with others. I also share many of my personal stories revealing how I got it wrong many times in the past and how I grew from front-line factory worker to become a Motivational Leadership Speaker.

INTRODUCTION

When You Increase Your Influence, You Increase Your Options.

"Leadership is influence. Nothing more. Nothing less. Everything rises and falls on leadership." ~ *John C. Maxwell*

Everyone is born a leader. However, everyone is not born a high impact leader.

I haven't always believed everyone is a leader. You may or may not at this point. That's okay. There is a lot to learn about leadership.

At this very moment, you may already be thinking to yourself, *"I'm not a leader."* My goal is to help you understand why everyone is a leader and to help you develop a deeper understanding of the principles of leadership and influence.

Developing a deep understanding of leadership has changed my life for the better. It has also changed the lives of my family members, friends, associates, and clients. My intention is to help you improve not only your life, but also the lives of those around you.

Until I became a student of leadership in 2008 which eventually led me to become a John Maxwell Certified Leadership Coach, Trainer, and Speaker in 2012, I did not understand leadership or realize everyone can benefit from learning the related principles.

In the past, I thought leadership was a term associated with being the boss and having formal authority over others. Those people are definitely leaders. But, I had been missing something. All of the other seven billion people on the planet are leaders too.

I say everyone is born a leader because I agree with John Maxwell, *"Leadership is Influence. Nothing more. Nothing less."* Everyone has influence. It's a fact. Therefore, everyone is a leader.

No matter your age, gender, religion, race, nationality, location, or position, everyone has influence. Whether you want to be a leader or not, you are. After reading this book, I hope you do not question whether or not you are a leader. However, I do hope you question what type of leader you are and what you need to do to increase your influence.

Everyone does not have authority, but everyone does have influence. There are plenty of examples in the world of people without authority leading people through influence alone. Actually, every one of us is an example. We have already done it. We know it is true. This principle is self-evident which means it contains its own evidence and does not need to be demonstrated or explained; it is obvious to everyone: we all have influence with others.

As I mentioned, the question to ask yourself is not, *"Am I a leader?"* The question to ask yourself is, *"What type of leader am I?"* The answer: whatever kind you choose to be. Choosing not to be a leader is not an option. As long as you live, you will have influence. You are a leader.

You started influencing your parents before you were actually born. You may have influence after your death. How? Thomas Edison still influences the world every time a light is turned on, you may do things in your life to influence others long after you're gone. Or, you may pass away with few people noticing. It depends on the choices you make.

Even when you're alone, you have influence.

The most important person you will ever influence is yourself. The degree to which you influence yourself determines the level of influence you ultimately have with others. Typically, when we are talking about leading ourselves, the word most commonly used to describe self-leadership is discipline which can be defined as giving yourself a command and following through with it. We must practice discipline daily to increase our influence with others.

"We must all suffer one of two things: the pain of discipline or the pain of regret or disappointment." ~ Jim Rohn

As I define leadership as influence, keep in mind the words leadership and influence can be interchanged anytime and anywhere. They are one and the same. Throughout this book, I'll help you remember by placing one of the words in parentheses next to the other occasionally as a reminder. They are synonyms. When you read one, think of the other.

Everything rises and falls on influence (leadership). When you share what you're learning, clearly define leadership as influence for others. They need to understand the context of what you are teaching and understand they *are* leaders (people with influence) too. If you truly want to learn and apply leadership principles, you must start teaching this material to others within 24-48 hours of learning it yourself.

You will learn the foundational principles of leadership (influence) which will help you understand the importance of the following five questions. You will be able to take effective action by growing yourself and possibly others to a higher level of leadership (influence). Everything you ever achieve, internally and externally, will be a direct result of your influence.

1. ***Why* do we influence?** – Our character determines *why* we influence. Who we are on the inside is what matters. Do we manipulate or motivate? It's all about our intent.

2. ***How* do we influence?** – Our character, combined with our competency, determines *how* we influence. Who we are and what we know combine to create our unique style of influence which determines our methods of influence.

3. ***Where* do we influence?** – Our passion and purpose determine *where* we have the greatest influence. What motivates and inspires us gives us the energy and authenticity to motivate and inspire others.

4. ***Who* do we influence?** – We influence those *who* buy-in to us. Only those valuing and seeking what we value and seek will volunteer to follow us. They give us or deny us permission to influence them based on how well we have developed our character and competency.

5. **When do we influence?** – We influence others *when* they want our influence. We choose when others influence us. Everyone else has the same choice. They decide when to accept or reject our influence.

The first three questions are about the choices we make as we lead (influence) ourselves and others. The last two questions deal more with the choices others will make as they decide first, *if* they will follow us, and second, *when* they will follow us. They will base their choices on *who we are* and *what we know*.

Asking these questions is important. Knowing the answers is more important. But, taking action based on the answers is most important. Cumulatively, the answers to these questions determine our leadership style and our level of influence (leadership).

On a scale of 1-10, your influence can be very low level (1) to very high level (10). But make no mistake, you *are* a leader. You *are* always on the scale. There is a positive and negative scale too. The higher on the scale you are the more effective you are. You will be at different levels with different people at different times depending on many different variables.

Someone thinking they are not a leader or someone that doesn't want to be a leader is still a leader. They will simply remain a low impact leader with low level influence getting low level results. They will likely spend much time frustrated with many areas of their life. Although they could influence a change, they choose instead to be primarily influenced by others.

What separates high impact leaders from low impact leaders? There are many things, but two primary differences are:

1) High impact leaders accept more responsibility in all areas of their lives while low impact leaders tend to blame others and transfer responsibility more often.

2) High impact leaders have more positive influence while low impact leaders tend to have more negative influence.

My passion has led me to grow into my purpose which is to help others increase their influence personally and professionally while setting and reaching their goals. I am very passionate and have great conviction. I have realized many benefits by getting better results in all areas of my life. I have improved relationships with my family members, my friends, my associates, my peers, and my clients. I have witnessed people within these same groups embrace leadership principles and reap the same benefits.

The degree to which I *live* what I teach determines my effectiveness. My goal is to learn it, live it, and *then* teach it. I had major internal struggles as I grew my way to where I am. I'm a long way from perfect, so I seek daily improvement. Too often, I see people teaching leadership but not living what they're teaching. If I teach it, I live it.

My goal is to be a better leader tomorrow than I am today. I simply must get out of my own way and lead. I must lead me effectively before I can lead others effectively, not only with acquired knowledge, but also with experience from applying and living the principles.

I'll be transparent with personal stories to help you see how I have applied leadership principles by sharing: How I've struggled. How I've learned. How I've sacrificed. And, how I've succeeded.

Go beyond highlighting or underlining key points. Take the time to write down your thoughts related to the principle. Write down what you want to change. Write down how you can apply the principle in your life. You may want to consider getting a journal to fully capture your thoughts as you progress through the chapters. What you are thinking as you read is often much more important than what you're reading.

Most importantly, do not focus your thoughts on others. Yes, they need it too. We all need it. I need it. You need it. However, if you focus outside of yourself, you are missing the very point. Your influence comes from within. Your influence rises and falls based on your choices. You have untapped and unlimited potential waiting to be released. Only you can release it.

You, like everyone else, were born a leader. Now, let's take a leadership journey together.

(If you enjoyed this Introduction to *Defining Influence*, it is available in paperback, audio, and as an eBook on Amazon.com)

Excerpt from

10 Values of High Impact Leaders

Our values are the foundation upon which we build our character. I'll be sharing 10 values high impact leaders work to master because they know these values will have a tremendous impact on their ability to lead others well. You may be thinking, *"Aren't there more than 10 leadership values?"* Absolutely! They seem to be endless. And, they are all important. These are simply 10 key values which I have chosen to highlight.

Since leadership is very dynamic and complex, the more values you have been able to internalize and utilize synergistically together, the more effective you will be. The more influence you will have.

"High performing organizations that continuously invest in leadership development are now defining new 21st century leadership models to deal with today's gaps in their leadership pipelines and the new global business environment. These people-focused organizations have generated nearly 60% improved business growth, reported a 66% improvement in bench strength, and showed a 62% improvement in employee retention. And, our research shows that it is not enough to just spend money on leadership training, but rather to follow specific practices that drive accelerated business results." ~ Josh Bersin

Do you want to become a high impact leader?

I believe everyone is a leader, but they are leading at different levels.

I believe everyone can and should lead from *where they are.*

I believe everyone can and should make a high impact.

I believe growth doesn't just happen; we must make it happen.

I believe before you will invest in yourself you must first believe in yourself.

I believe leaders must believe in their team before they will invest in their team.

I truly believe *everything rises and falls on influence.*

There is a story of a tourist who paused for a rest in a small town in the mountains. He went over to an old man sitting on a bench in front of the only store in town and inquired, *"Friend, can you tell me something this town is noted for?"*

"Well," replied the old man, *"I don't rightly know except it's the starting point to the world. You can start here and go anywhere you want."* [1]

That's a great little story. We are all at *"the starting point"* to the world, and we *"can start here and go anywhere we want."* We can expand our influence 360° in all directions by starting in the center with ourselves.

Consider the following illustration. Imagine you are standing in the center. You can make a high impact. However, it will not happen by accident. You must become intentional. You must live with purpose while focusing on your performance as you develop your potential.

Note: Illustration and 10 Values are listed on the following pages.

Why we do what we do is about our *purpose.*

How we do what we do is about our *performance.*

What we do will determine our *potential.*

Where these three components overlap, you will achieve a
HIGH IMPACT.

10 Values of High Impact Leaders

1

THE VALUE OF VISION
Vision is the foundation of hope.
"When there's hope in the future, there's power in the present." ~ Les Brown

2

THE VALUE OF MODELING
Someone is always watching you.
"Who we are on the inside is what people see on the outside." ~ Mack Story

3

THE VALUE OF RESPONSIBILITY
When we take responsibility, we take control.
"What is common sense is not always common practice." ~ Stephen R. Covey

4

THE VALUE OF TIMING
It matters when you do what you do.
"It's about doing the right thing for the right reason at the right time." ~ Mack Story

5

THE VALUE OF RESPECT
To be respected, we must be respectful.
"Go See, ask why, and show respect"
~ Jim Womack

6

THE VALUE OF EMPOWERMENT
Leaders gain influence by
giving it to others.
"Leadership is not reserved for leaders."
~ Marcus Buckingham

7

THE VALUE OF DELEGATION
We should lead with questions
instead of directions.
"Delegation 101: Delegating 'what to do,' makes
you responsible. Delegating 'what to accomplish,'
allows others to become responsible."
~ Mack Story

8

THE VALUE OF MULTIPLICATION
None of us is as influential as all of us.
"To add growth, lead followers. To multiply, lead
leaders." ~ John C. Maxwell

9

THE VALUE OF RESULTS
Leaders like to make things happen.
"Most people fail in the getting started."
~ Maureen Falcone

10

THE VALUE OF SIGNIFICANCE
Are you going to settle for success?
"Significance is a choice that only successful people can make."
~ Mack Story

Excerpt (Chapter 3 of 30) from
__Blue-Collar Leadership__® __& Culture:__
The 5 Components for Building High Performance Teams

THE IMPACT OF CULTURE

THOSE WHO WORK THERE WILL DETERMINE WHO WANTS TO WORK THERE

"I think the most important and difficult thing is to create a culture in the organization where leadership is really important. It's important for people in the company to realize that this is a growth-oriented company, and the biggest thing we have to grow here is you, because it's you who will make this company better by your own growth. ~ Jim Blanchard

Listen to the voices of leaders who are losing the labor war:

- "We just can't find any good people."
    As if…there aren't any good or great people.
- "Due to the low unemployment rate, there just aren't any good people left."
    As if…the only people who can be offered a job are those without a job.
- "In today's labor market, those who want to work are already working."
    As if…those who are working at one place can't decide to work at a different place.
- "When we do get good people, they won't stay."
    As if…the problem is always with the people and never with their leaders.

One thing I know about leaders who make these and similar comments is this: Their culture is a competitive disadvantage. Someone else has the advantage and is winning the battle for the good and great people. The good and great people certainly aren't out of work wishing they had a job. They're working someplace else.

Until a leader is aware of the problem, they can't address the problem. In case it's not obvious, the problem is their culture. The leader owns this problem whether they want to or not. Every time I hear these comments, and I hear them a lot, I know I'm talking to a leader who doesn't know what they don't know.

Ria and I hear leaders across varying blue-collar and white-collar industries repeatedly making these comments as we travel across the USA speaking on leadership development. These voices seem to be getting louder and louder. In fact, these voices are an inspiration for this book.

There are many leaders in blue-collar industries needing help. I want to help them stop searching for good people and start attracting great people. The transformation won't happen overnight. However, until it starts happening, it's not going to happen. My intention is to use this book to raise awareness while providing a transformational road map for those leaders who want to make their culture their greatest competitive advantage.

We were speaking in Louisville, KY recently to owners of blue-collar organizations. Afterward, one approached and said, "There isn't a magic pill is there? I think we all hoped there was." I replied, "No sir. There isn't a magic pill or an easy button. This is how you build a high performance team and an exceptional culture that will attract, retain, and support them. There is no other way."

Your culture is always attracting certain types of people and repelling others. Who we are is who we attract. This principle applies to individuals as well as organizations. The culture within your organization is negatively or positively impacting those within the organization, and some who are outside the organization.

The key point is to understand the people inside your organization are constantly providing the most influential type of advertising about your organization and the leaders within it. It's called word of mouth advertising. How your team is feeling inside the organization will determine what they're saying outside the organization.

If what they're saying about their leaders and the organization to others is good, it'll be easier to find good people. If what they're saying is great, it'll be easier to attract great people. But, if what they're saying is bad, finding good people will be hard, if not impossible.

Remember the voices at the start of this chapter? Those leaders had team members who were sharing bad word of mouth advertising about the organization. Unless those leaders choose to change, nothing will change.

Common sense reveals it's easier to win the labor war while attracting great people instead of searching for good people. However, what's common sense isn't always common practice. Often, it takes uncommon sense to act on things that are commonly understood. Creating an organizational culture that will attract and retain great people requires leaders with uncommon sense.

The best led companies aren't impacted by labor shortages because they're consistently attracting the best and the brightest people to their organizations.

"If we lose sight of people, we lose sight of the very purpose of leadership." ~ Tony Dungy

Excerpt (Trait 4 of 30) from
Blue-Collar Leadership® & Teamwork:
30 Traits of High Impact Players

BE RESPONSIBLE

MAKING THIS CHOICE GIVES YOU A VOICE

"Total responsibility for failure is a difficult thing to accept, and taking ownership when things go wrong requires extraordinary humility and courage."
~ Jocko Willink

The higher we climb up the organizational chart or the higher we climb up the pay scale, the harder it is for many of us to remain humble. However, as high impact team players, it's our responsibility to choose to be humble regardless of our status or income. And if necessary, it's also our responsibility to learn what it truly means to be humble.

Humility is a choice that high impact players will make.

If you haven't accomplished much or done much, it's a little easier to remain humble. I believe as a whole the blue-collar workforce is naturally more humble simply because of who we are and where we come from. However, I also believe some who climb their way up from the entry-level positions let it go to their heads.

I want to remain a humble high impact player. That's on me. Not letting my success go to my head is my responsibility. I've also gone a step farther and made helping others do the same my responsibility. High impact team players always do more than is required.

Each of us is responsible for choosing our values and

those values will determine our circumstances and the impact we have, especially when it comes to teamwork.

Just as humility is sometimes a hard choice for those with a high position or status, taking responsibility is often a hard choice for those in a low position or status. But as I've learned over the years, taking responsibility seems to be a hard choice for many regardless of their title, position, rank, status, or income.

When it comes to teamwork, low impact players dodge responsibility like it's a deadly disease. They may disappear when the task is being addressed or begin to make excuses as to why they can't help and shouldn't be asked to help. That creates distrust.

High impact players know a secret: When low impact players are whining, it's easy to start shining. They also know how to shine. It's actually pretty simple. They just listen for whining, and then step up and say, "I'll do it."

At that moment, the high impact player builds trust by simply taking the responsibility. The next responsibility of the high impact player is to follow through and get results. If they don't, they will create distrust with the team and the leaders. If they do, they will build additional trust with the team and the leaders.

Leaders are ultimately responsible for making things happen. If they don't make things happen, it won't be long before they are replaced by someone else who will be given the same mission. High impact players know the quickest way to build trust with a leader is to help them get results, so that's what they focus on doing.

As they develop a reputation for helping the leaders get results, their influence increases with those leaders. Because of their choice (taking responsibility and following through), they earn a voice. As time passes, the high impact players are asked their opinions much more often than the low impact players.

As a result, the high impact players begin to influence the leader's choices and the team's direction. They're still on the team, but they're playing at much higher level. Those who are willing to make things happen are also given more chances to make things happen.

High impact players are never just along for the ride. They want to drive. They see the big picture. They don't shy away from responsibility. They wake up everyday looking for an opportunity to shine.

Imagine a team full of low impact players where everyone is dodging responsibility on every front. The leader will be frustrated, and the team will be frustrated. And little, if anything, will get accomplished. Unfortunately, these types of teams are common. Depending on your circumstances, it may be too easy to imagine this team. If so, don't miss what's right in front of you: endless opportunities to shine.

Now imagine a very different team, one filled with high impact players. They could be given the exact same mission as the frustrated low impact team. However, no one would be frustrated. The mission would be accomplished. Instead of being focused on finding excuses, the entire team would be focused on finding a way to make it happen. In that case, everyone shines.

What's the major difference between the two teams above? Attitude. Low impact players tend to have a negative attitude. High impact players always have a positive attitude. Attitude is a choice. If we can choose to be positive or negative, why not choose to be positive.

"Responsibility includes two important ideas – choosing right over wrong and accepting ownership for one's conduct and obligations." ~ Charles G. Koch

Excerpt (Ch. 4 of 30) from
Blue-Collar Leadership® & Supervision:
Unleash Your Team's Potential

UNDERSTANDING ARTIFICIAL INFLUENCE

THERE IS A DIFFERENCE BETWEEN SOMEONE RESPECTING YOUR POSITION AND SOMEONE RESPECTING YOU

"Into the hands of every individual is given a marvelous power for good or evil - the silent, unconscious, unseen influence of his life. This is simply the constant radiation of what man really is, not what he pretends to be."
~ William George Jordan

If you want to begin to lead beyond your position, you must be respected by those you want to influence. No one gives you respect. You can demand respect all day long, but it's a waste of time. I always laugh (on the inside) when I hear someone demand respect. You will never be respected because you demand to be respected, at work or at home. It's simply not going to happen.

Think about it from your own point of view. If there's a boss or manager you don't like because of who they are as a person, can they demand respect from you and get it? Absolutely not. You may respect their position. But, you will never respect them simply because they demand it. You *must* respect their position to *keep* your job. But, you don't have to respect *them* to keep your job.

A position will give you authority but not influence. Influence must be earned by first earning respect. The more you are respected the more influence you will gain. Everything I'm sharing in this book, *if applied*, will help you earn respect and increase your influence with others.

Having a position or title such as Mom, Dad, Coach, Boss, Supervisor, Manager, VP, President, CEO, Owner, etc. gives you authority and control over other people. I call this *artificial influence*. Artificial influence creates the *illusion* that you have *real* influence. However, if you choose to influence people using only artificial influence, you are not leading. You are simply managing. Sure you may accomplish a lot, but what are you leaving on the table?

You can easily validate the principle of artificial influence by considering those bosses you've had, or now have, that you would never follow if they didn't control your pay, your time off, your promotions, etc. If you only follow a boss because you *have to*, their influence is *not* real. It's artificial. And unfortunately for the company, most likely, you will only do what you have to do.

The title of boss is one that is simply given, often by another manager with artificial influence. However, when it comes to real influence, managers are not in the same league as leaders. If you develop real influence based on character-based principles that you have internalized, then you will *earn* the right to lead. When you do, those reporting to you will do much *more than they have to* simply because they *respect* you.

A high impact leader operates from a position of real influence, not artificial influence or authority.

Listen to the voices of those with *artificial* influence:

- How am I supposed to make something happen when those people don't report to me?
- I can't make them do anything. They don't report to me and won't do anything I tell them to do.
- I can't get anything done in that department. They report to someone else, not me. It's useless to try.
- How can I be responsible for their results when they don't report to me?
- If you want me to make it happen, you've got to give me authority over those people.
- My hands are tied. They don't report to me.

Phrases like those are always spoken by a manager, never

by a leader. I've heard them spoken many times in my career by managers who don't have a clue about leadership. The only influence they have at work is directly tied to the authority, *artificial influence*, which is associated with the position they hold. Without it, they wouldn't accomplish much of anything.

I remember being in a facility as a consultant once. I needed some help from a few team members in a different department, so I asked the manager I was working with if it would be okay if I went over and asked them for some help. He said, *"You'll have to wait. I'll have to get an interpreter because none of them speak English."* I said, *"Okay, I'll go wait over there."* I thought it was interesting. When I got there, they all spoke English to me. Leadership is influence.

Managers make things happen with people who *have to* help them. Leaders make things happen with people who *want to* help them.

Most managers have never read a leadership book and can't understand a leader doesn't need authority to make something happen. Leaders only need *influence* to make something happen. Leadership is *not* about who *has* to help you. Leadership *is* about who *wants* to help you.

Research studies have repeatedly shown a 40% productivity increase when comparing people who *want to* follow a leader with those who *have to* follow a manager.

A manager thrives on artificial influence and is not interested in developing himself or others in order to capture this massive loss of productivity. That's what leaders do, not managers.

How do you influence? What is your style? Are you a director or a connector? Do you tell or sell? What would change if you had more real influence in every situation?

"When we look at people who disobey their leaders, the first question we ought to ask is not, 'What's wrong with those people?' but rather, 'What's wrong with their leader?' It says that responsibility begins at the top."
~ Malcolm Gladwell

Excerpt (Ch. 26 of 30) from
Blue-Collar Kaizen:
Leading Lean & Lean Teams

LEVERAGE THE TEAM

FOCUS ON STRENGTHS;
DEVELOP WEAKNESSES

"Instead of focusing on weaknesses, give your
attention to people's strengths. Focus on sharpening
skills that already exist. Compliment positive qualities.
Bring out the gifts inherent in them. Weaknesses can
wait unless they are character flaws. Only after you
have developed a strong rapport with the person and
they have begun to grow and gain confidence should
you address areas of weakness...and then those
should be handled gently and one at a time."
~ John C. Maxwell

High impact Lean leaders have a gift for turning a
group of people into a team in a short period of time.

At the start of a kaizen event, calling the group of
people a team is a poor use of the word team. They are
simply a group of people assembled in a room about to
be given a task to accomplish together. Most often, some
want to be there, and some don't want to be there. Odds
are, this specific group of people has never worked
together on a project before.

Knowing about continuous improvement is a must if
you're going to lead a kaizen event. However, knowing
about continuous improvement (your competency) will
not be the key to turning a group of people into a team of
people. Turning a group of people into a team of people

is about having respect for the people. Your ability to quickly build a strong, functional team will be determined primarily by your character and secondarily by your competency. Your character is key in this area.

I've seen some very talented Lean leaders and others who have an extensive in-depth knowledge of Lean attempt to lead kaizen events. Most often, they struggle from the moment the event kicks off until the end. They know a lot about Lean but very little about leading people effectively. Why? Because their focus has been on learning Lean, not on learning leadership.

When it comes to growing, developing, and creating a new team, high impact Lean leaders know to focus on the team member's strengths in their area of competency and to develop their weaknesses in the area of character.

Each team member's competency strengths (what they know and can do), if leveraged, will launch the team forward. Each team member's character weaknesses (who they are) will hold the team back. This includes you.

High impact Lean leaders know there are always character issues. We all have them. A few of us are constantly working to improving ourselves, but many of us aren't. Focusing on character weaknesses is why high impact Lean leaders blend leadership development and personal growth components into all of their continuous improvement initiatives.

This is why I utilize the 20/80 rule I taught you in chapter 19. I didn't start using it by accident. I started using it by design. Until then, I only focused on leveraging the team's strengths. But, I hadn't been focused on developing their weaknesses. I'm sure you already know the root cause of most major problems that arise during kaizen events, whether with team members or people not on the team, is rooted in character issues.

The majority of Lean leaders focus only on the continuous improvement (competency) component of Lean. As a result, they provide no leadership in the area that will hold them and the team back the most, character development.

The reason Lean leaders do not address character development during kaizen events is because many of them are not addressing it in their own lives. In other words, because they are not leading themselves well, they cannot lead others well. Character development is always the missing link personally and professionally.

In the area of competency, ask questions and generate discussions to find out what people like or don't like to do. Don't assume they like to do what they are paid to do. I always have everyone introduce and speak about themselves before I talk about anything. I ask what their job is, how long they have been with the organization, what their previous job was, what their hobbies are, what they do for fun, how much Lean and event experience they have, and I ask them to tell me about their family.

The answers to these questions and the associated discussions allow me to connect and learn about their strengths. Then, I'm positioned to leverage the team.

"Humility means knowing and using your strength for the benefit of others, on behalf of a higher purpose. The humble leader is not weak, but strong...is not preoccupied with self, but with how best to use his or her strengths for the good of others. A humble leader does not think less of himself, but chooses to consider the needs of others in fulfilling a worthy cause. We love to be in the presence of a humble leader because they bring out the very best in us. Their focus is on our purpose, our contribution, and our ability to accomplish all we set out to accomplish." ~ Alan Ross

Excerpt (Toolbox Tip #15) from
Blue-Collar Leadership® Toolbox Tips:
60 Micro-Lessons to Maximize Your INFLUENCE

🔧 Toolbox Tip #15

Character counts. Who we are on the inside determines what others see, feel, and experience on the outside.

Why It Matters: When it comes to character, it's not about what we know. It's about who we are. People are most often hired for what they know, but they are most often fired for who they are. Our character will either launch us or limit us. Character is personal, but it's not private.

What We Do: We intentionally make choices that reveal a high degree of character. We make and keep commitments. We do what we said we would do, when we said we would do it, how we said we would do it, because we said we would do it. We ensure our motive, agenda, and behavior are aligned with positive, character-based principles. We say and do things that build trust.

What We Don't Do: We don't lie. We don't make and break commitments. We don't talk about others behind their backs. We don't fail to stand for what's right. We don't hang around negative people. We don't do or say things that create distrust.

Bad Example(s): Blaming others for our behavior when things don't go our way. Speaking to others in anger. Pretending to know when we don't know.

Think About This

"Our reputations do not come from how we talk about ourselves. Our reputations come from how others talk about us." ~ Simon Sinek

Allowing our pride and ego to prevent us from doing the right thing.

Ask Yourself: Do I ever blame others for my behavior? Do others control me, or do I control me? Who is responsible for my behavior? What does my behavior communicate to others?

What Do You Think?

Order books online at Amazon or TopStoryLeadership.com

High impact leaders align their habits with key values in order to maximize their influence. High impact leaders intentionally grow and develop themselves in an effort to more effectively grow and develop others.

These *10 Values* are commonly understood. However, they are not always commonly practiced. These *10 Values* will help you build trust and accelerate relationship building. Those mastering these *10 Values* will be able to lead with speed as they develop 360° of influence from wherever they are.

Order books online at Amazon or TopStoryLeadership.com

Are you looking for transformation in your life? Do you want better results? Do you want stronger relationships?

In *Defining Influence*, Mack breaks down many of the principles that will allow anyone at any level to methodically and intentionally increase their positive influence.

Mack blends his personal growth journey with lessons on the principles he learned along the way. He's not telling you what he learned after years of research, but rather what he learned from years of application and transformation. Everything rises and falls on influence.

Order books online at Amazon or TopStoryLeadership.com

10 Foundational Elements of Intentional Transformation serves as a source of motivation and inspiration to help you climb your way to the next level and beyond as you learn to intentionally create a better future for yourself. The pages will ENCOURAGE, ENGAGE, and EMPOWER you as you become more focused and intentional about moving from where you are to where you want to be.

All of us are somewhere, but most of us want to be somewhere else. However, we don't always know how to get there. You will learn how to intentionally move forward as you learn to navigate the 10 foundational layers of transformation.

Order books online at Amazon or TopStoryLeadership.com

"Sales persuasion and influence, moving others, has changed more in the last 10 years than it has in the last 100 years. It has transitioned from buyer beware to seller beware" ~ Daniel Pink

So, it's no longer *"Buyer beware!"* It's *"Seller beware!"* Why? Today, the buyer has the advantage over the seller. Most often, they are holding it in their hand. It's a smart phone. They can learn everything about your product before they meet you. They can compare features and prices instantly. The major advantage you do still have is: YOU! IF they like you. IF they trust you. IF they feel you want to help them.

This book is filled with 30 short chapters providing unique insights that will give you the advantage, not over the buyer, but over your competition: those who are selling what you're selling. It will help you sell yourself.

Order books online at Amazon or BlueCollarLeadership.com

It's easier to compete when you're attracting great people instead of searching for good people.

Blue-Collar Leadership® & Culture will help you understand why culture is the key to becoming a sought after employer of choice within your industry and in your area of operation.

You'll also discover how to leverage the components of The Transformation Equation to create a culture that will support, attract, and retain high performance team members.

Blue-Collar Leadership® & Culture is intended to serve as a tool, a guide, and a transformational road map for leaders who want to create a high impact culture that will become their greatest competitive advantage.

124

Order books online at Amazon or BlueCollarLeadership.com

(Also available in Spanish)

Are you ready to play at the next level and beyond?

In today's high stakes game of business, the players on the team are the competitive advantage for any organization. But, only if they are on the field instead of on the bench.

The competitive advantage for every individual is developing 360° of influence regardless of position, title, or rank.

Blue-Collar Leadership® & Teamwork provides a simple, yet powerful and unique, resource for individuals who want to increase their influence and make a high impact. It's also a resource and tool for leaders, teams, and organizations, who are ready to Engage the Front Line to Improve the Bottom Line.

Order books online at Amazon or BlueCollarLeadership.com

"I wish someone would have given me these books 30 years ago when I started my career on the front lines. They would have launched my career then. They can launch your career now." ~ *Mack Story*

Blue-Collar Leadership® and *Blue-Collar Leadership*® *& Supervision* were written specifically for those working on the front lines and those who are leading them. With 30 short, easy to read 3 page chapters, these books contain powerful, yet simple to understand leadership principles and lessons.

Note: These two Blue-Collar Leadership® *books are the blue-collar version of the MAXIMIZE books and contain nearly identical content.*

Download the first 5 chapters of these books FREE at: BlueCollarLeadership.com/download

Order books online at Amazon or BlueCollarLeadership.com

QUICKLY DEVELOP LEADERS AT EVERY LEVEL

Leaders are BUSY. That's why Mack Story designed *Toolbox Tips*, a collection of powerful leadership principles delivered in a short and easy to understand format for *quick* and *consistent* workforce development.

Kick-off weekly meetings by reviewing a *Toolbox Tip* on **responsibility**, start your team safety meetings with a *Toolbox Tip* on **trust**, or begin your management team meeting with a *Toolbox Tip* on **character**.

Leverage the power of micro-learning with powerful, common-sense leadership principles. Quickly and consistently review, discuss, and apply *Toolbox Tips* to create a leadership culture filled with high impact individuals, high impact team players, and high impact leaders worth following.

Order books online at Amazon or BlueCollarLeadership.com

The biggest challenge in process improvement and cultural transformation isn't identifying the problems. It's execution: implementing and sustaining the solutions.

Blue-Collar Kaizen is a resource for anyone in any position who is, or will be, leading a team through process improvement and change. Learn to engage, empower, and encourage your team for long term buy-in and sustained gains.

Mack Story has over 11,000 hours experience leading hundreds of leaders and thousands of their cross-functional kaizen team members through process improvement, organizational change, and cultural transformation. He shares lessons learned from his experience and many years of studying, teaching, and applying leadership principles.

Order books online at Amazon or TopStoryLeadership.com

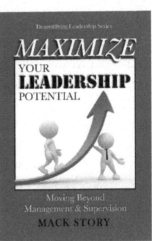

"I wish someone had given me these books 30 years ago when I started my career. They would have changed my life then. They can change your life now." ~ Mack Story

MAXIMIZE Your Potential will help you learn to lead yourself well. *MAXIMIZE Your Leadership Potential* will help you learn to lead others well. With 30 short, easy to read 3 page chapters, these books contain simple and easy to understand, yet powerful leadership lessons.

Note: These two MAXIMIZE books are the white-collar, or non-specific, version of the Blue-Collar Leadership® books and contain nearly identical content.

ABOUT RIA STORY

Mack's wife, Ria, is also a motivational leadership speaker, author, and a world class coach who has a unique ability to help people develop and achieve their life and career goals and guide them in building the habits and discipline to achieve their personal view of greatness. Ria brings a wealth of personal experience in working with clients to achieve their personal goals and aspirations in a way few coaches can.

Like many, Ria has faced adversity in life. Raised on an isolated farm in Alabama, she suffered extreme sexual abuse by her father from age 12 to 19. Desperate to escape, she left home at 19 without a job, a car, or even a high school diploma. Ria learned to be resilient, and not just survive, but thrive. (Watch her 7 minute TEDx talk at RiaStory.com/TEDx) She worked her way through school, acquiring an MBA with a 4.0 GPA, and eventually resigned from her career in the corporate world to pursue a passion for helping others achieve success.

Ria's background includes more than 10 years in healthcare administration, including several years in management, and later, Director of Compliance and Regulatory Affairs for a large healthcare organization. Ria's responsibilities included oversight of thousands of organizational policies, organizational compliance with all State and Federal regulations, and responsibility for several million dollars in Medicare appeals.

Ria co-founded Top Story Leadership, which offers leadership speaking, training, coaching, and consulting.

Ria's Story From Ashes To Beauty
by Ria Story

The unforgettable story and inspirational memoir of a young woman who was extremely sexually abused by her father from age 12 to 19 and then rejected by her mother. (Watch 7 minutes of her story in her TEDx talk at RiaStory.com/TEDx)

For the first time, Ria publicly reveals details of the extreme sexual abuse she endured growing up. 13 years after leaving home at 19, she decided to speak out about her story and encourage others to find hope and healing.

Determined to not only survive, but also thrive, Ria shares how she was able to overcome the odds and find hope and healing to Achieve Abundant Life. She shares the leadership principles she applied to find professional success, personal significance, and details how she was able to find the courage to share her story to give hope to others around the world.

Ria states, *"It would be easier for me to let this story go untold forever and simply move on with life…One of the most difficult things I've ever done is write this book. Victims of sexual assault or abuse don't want to talk because they want to avoid the social stigma and the fear of not being believed or the possibility of being blamed for something that was not their fault. My hope and prayer is someone will benefit from learning how I was able to overcome such difficult circumstances. That brings purpose to the pain and reason enough to share what I would rather have left behind forever. Our scars make us stronger."*

Available at Amazon.com in paperback, audio, and eBook. To order your signed copy, to learn more about Ria, or to book her to speak at your event, please visit: RiaStory.com/TEDx

Order books online at Amazon or
RiaStory.com

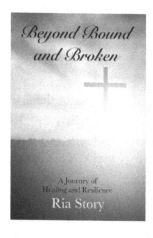

Ria Story

In *Beyond Bound and Broken*, Ria shares how she overcame the shame, fear, and doubt she developed after enduring years of extreme sexual abuse by her father. Forced to play the role of a wife and even shared with other men due to her father's perversions, Ria left home at 19 without a job, a car, or even a high-school diploma. This book also contains lessons on resilience and overcoming adversity that you can apply to your own life.

In *Ria's Story From Ashes To Beauty*, Ria tells her personal story of growing up as a victim of extreme sexual abuse from age 12 – 19, leaving home to escape, and her decision to tell her story. She shares her heart in an attempt to help others overcome their own adversity.

Order books online at Amazon or RiaStory.com

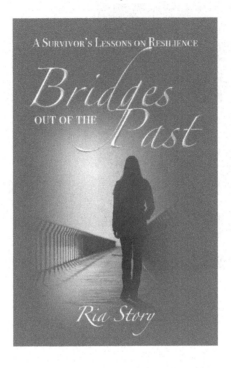

It's not what happens to you in life. It's who you become because of it. We all experience pain, grief, and loss in life. Resilience is the difference between *"I didn't die,"* and *"I learned to live again."* In this captivating book on resilience, Ria walks you through her own horrific story of more than seven years of sexual abuse by her father. She then shares how she learned not only to survive, but also to thrive in spite of her past. Learn how to overcome challenges, obstacles, and adversity in your own life by building a bridge out of the past and into the future.

(Watch 7 minutes of her story at RiaStory.com/TEDx)

Order books online at Amazon or RiaStory.com

You have untapped potential to do, have, and be more in life. But, developing your potential and becoming the best version of yourself will require personal transformation. You will have to transform from who you are today into who you want to become tomorrow.

Gain unique insight in, *"Fearfully and Wonderfully Me: Become the Woman You are Destined to Be"* and the accompanying workbook to help you: believe in yourself and your potential; embrace your self-worth; overcome self-limiting beliefs; increase your influence personally & professionally; and achieve your goals & develop a mindset for success. These two resources will empower you to own your story, write a new chapter, and become the woman and leader you are destined to be.

Order books online at Amazon or RiaStory.com

You have untapped potential waiting to be unlocked. To be successful requires us to have knowledge of the principles of success, awareness of how to utilize them, and discipline to intentionally apply them. There are no shortcuts to success, but we can travel much faster when we have an achievement model we can apply. This model will help you develop more influence personally and professionally, execute an action plan for personal success, and maximize your potential in life. Both women and men alike will find practical and relevant information to immediately apply to their situation and improve the outcome.

Order books online at Amazon or RiaStory.com

Note: Leadership Gems is the generic, non-gender specific, version of Leadership Gems for Women. The content is very similar.

Women are naturally high level leaders because they are relationship oriented. However, it's a *"man's world"* out there and natural ability isn't enough to help you be successful as a leader. You must be intentional.

Ria packed these books with 30 leadership gems which very successful people internalize and apply. Ria has combined her years of experience in leadership roles of different organizations along with years of studying, teaching, training, and speaking on leadership to give you these 30, short and simple, yet powerful and profound, lessons to help you become very successful, regardless of whether you are in a formal leadership position or not.

Order books online at Amazon or RiaStory.com

Become inspired by this 30-day collection of daily devotions for women, where you will find practical advice on intentionally living with a grateful heart, inspirational quotes, short journaling opportunities, and scripture from God's Word on practicing gratitude.

Motivational Planning Journals
Choose a theme for the season of your life!
Now available at Amazon.com or RiaStory.com

| Motivational | Purposeful/Living Your Legacy | Productivity |
| Joy/Faith | Resilience | Make the Most of Today |

Start each day with a purposeful mindset, and you will achieve your priorities based on your values.

Just a few minutes of intentional thought every morning will allow you to focus your energy, increase your influence, and make your day all that it can be!

Each journal in the series has different motivational quotes and a motivational theme. Choose one or get all six for an entire year's worth of **Motivational Planning**!

Order books online at Amazon or RiaStory.com

Ria's *Effective Leadership Series* books are written to develop and enhance your leadership skills, while also helping you increase your abilities in areas like communication and relationships, time management, planning and execution, leading and implementing change. Look for more books in the *Effective Leadership Series*:

- *Straight Talk: The Power of Effective Communication*

- *PRIME Time: The Power of Effective Planning*

- *Change Happens: Leading Yourself and Others through Change (Co-authored by Ria & Mack Story)*